CHINA'S COMMERCIAL SEXS

MW01046655

Rethinking Intimacy, Masculinity, and Criminal Justice

Exploring the experiences of both male clients and female sex workers, *China's Commercial Sexscapes* expands upon the complex dynamics of sex worker and client relationships and places these interactions within the wider implications of expanding globalization and capitalism.

The book is based in large part upon interviews with sex workers and their clients the author conducted while undercover as a bartender in Dongguan, an important industrial city in Guangdong province and an explicit, complicated, and multidimensional setting for study. In the wake of the financial crisis, the purchasing of sex by single, young-adult males has become an increasingly socially acceptable way for men to perform and experience heteronormative masculinity. Investigating human rights, social policy, and the criminal justice system in China, this book applies the concept of "edgework" to the commercial sex industry in Dongguan to study how men and women interact within the changing global economy.

EILEEN YUK-HA TSANG is an associate professor in the Department of Social and Behavioural Sciences at the City University of Hong Kong.

China's Commercial Sexscapes

Rethinking Intimacy, Masculinity, and Criminal Justice

EILEEN YUK-HA TSANG

UNIVERSITY OF TORONTO PRESS
Toronto Buffalo London

Contents

Part Four: Social Policy Implications and Criminal Justice

Acknowledgments

This is a story of my research journey. And like all research, it begins with the researcher and the interviewees. A researcher's interest in a certain phenomenon goes quite a long way in shaping the initial conception of what the research study is about. How that interest is framed necessarily reflects both the researcher's particular vantage point and his or her concerns, destinations, and motivations. I embraced an exciting research journey, and I owe thanks to many people who helped bring this book to fruition. Thanks are due, first and foremost, to my interviewees, whose willingness to speak frankly and openly about their struggles was inspiring. Their recollections provided a remarkable source of insight into urban sexscapes. We began as strangers and are now friends. The interviewees in this book provided the wonderful and deeply precious insights into their lives which helped carry me forward as an ethnographer. Although some have left China and now live overseas or in Hong Kong, I'm grateful that we continue to connect, share, and update each other through WeChat. Without their trust and help, this book would not have been possible. The exciting stories from my interviewees in the commercial sex industry keep my research journey ongoing and rocking.

A great debt also goes to my university classmates Henry, Kevin, and Ken for their friendship and help on this project. They made it possible for me to have access to a wide range of influential people across China. They went the extra mile to arrange transportation and accommodation for me and generally facilitated logistical matters during the course of my fieldwork. I will never forget how difficult it was to do the fieldwork in the three niche markets as well as among the streetwalkers. The police visited me many times, checking my travel documents and generally giving me a hard time. However, with the trust and support of Henry, Kevin, and Ken, I could gain access as an unpaid bartender to meet and talk candidly with those I sought. Thanks to their friendship and familiarity with both "underground" people and cadres, they made my fieldwork safer, smoother, and more promising than I ever expected. I owe them a great deal and am forever indebted to them.

I would also like to thank my husband, Jeff Wilkinson, who spent many hours in incisive conversation with me, listening to my ideas and suggesting how they might be presented more effectively. His no-nonsense approach to theoretical and practical research work continues to inspire. He has made countless sacrifices in his own life so that I could chase after my dream of writing this book. He had to get used to being without me weekends, holidays, and vacation breaks these past years. He has nourished me intellectually and emotionally and helped me to contemplate avenues of exploration that I would not otherwise have considered. I owe him for his support, comfort, laughter, and encouragement in the final throes of book writing. Finally, I am indebted to my parents for their support and forbearance. They had to get used to being without me for weekends, holiday, and vacation breaks as well.

This book also has a very special and important acknowledgment to my in-laws, Bob and Betty. With Bob's recent passing, I especially remember him. The first time I met Bob was in Melbourne, Florida, several years ago when Jeff and I drove over from Houston for Christmas. He greeted me at the door with a big smile and a loud "Welcome to Florida and Merry Christmas!" I came to learn he always wore a smile on his face. Perhaps that day he felt a little nervous about meeting this Chinese woman who seemed a strange mix of England, Hong Kong, and America yet did not fit entirely in any one culture. Still, my father-in-law was an amazing, irrepressible ball of light. He was energy and excitement. He was smart and resourceful, and he got things done. People who met him fell in love with him and his warm personality. He was a private person and delighted in being alone, working on genealogy or studying financial management. But wherever he went, he had a "hail fellow well met" demeanour. Whatever country he was in – around fifty was the final count – he bonded with the people there, because he respected them and cared about their well-being, and that care was reciprocated.

He was a person of superlatives. I love to cook and made garlic rolls for everyone to eat. Countless times I remember him saying, "This is the BEST garlic roll I ever had." I didn't know how true it was. However, when I saw his satisfaction, I believed him. I could not understand why he did not like my "king" dishes like chili chicken, rose chicken, Chinese soup, seafood, Chinese pudding, and Korean rice cakes with kimchi; he only loved my garlic rolls or bread. He was interested in the chemistry of baking. Although our time together was short, it was precious, and my memory and respect grow each day. I am so lucky that I did not experience his explosive temper, only his enthusiasm, kindness, and hospitality. He lived his life that way. Anything I did for him was deeply appreciated. He went into a coma in early September 2017 as massive Hurricane Irma bore down on them along the Florida coast and passed away as it washed over them. I know he will be at peace in the other world without pain and struggles. Therefore, I end by saying that my father-in-law is missed, and he always was, and is, the BEST. This book is dedicated to him.

CHINA'S COMMERCIAL SEXSCAPES

Rethinking Intimacy, Masculinity, and Criminal Justice

Introduction

This book is based on several in-depth interviews I conducted with sex workers and clients in Dongguan. Originally, this research was to be about something else. In the summer of 2009, I stood at the front gate of a garment factory in Dongguan, uncertain, yet determined to go inside. Massive jets of hot air blew unceasingly outward, engulfing me in oppressive dry heat. I had just finished a gruelling 13-hour flight from Birmingham, England, to Hong Kong, followed by several hours riding a train to this, my final destination. A friend of mine, Ray, owned a factory in Dongguan and had arranged for me to live and work there for four months so that I could immerse myself in a Chinese middle-class working environment. At the time, I was researching the Chinese middle class for my doctoral degree, and my specific fieldwork was to be in Dongguan, located in the heart of Guangdong province. Dongguan has attracted many foreigners since China joined the World Trade Organization in December 2001. It is an important industrial city of around three million inhabitants and a significant part of the 25 million-plus residents in the greater Pearl River Delta, which includes Guangzhou, Shenzhen, Macau, and Hong Kong (Phillips, 2013; He, 2014).

But many people there were facing hard times. The global economic recession of 2008 had bankrupted many factories, forcing people to scramble for alternative means of making a living. Sadly, countless numbers of young men and women turned to sexual services, which appeared under the guise of "easy money," and the city boasted countless clubs, bars, nightclubs, and massage parlours where the sex industry could flourish. The sex industry in Dongguan was estimated to employ between 500,000 and 800,000 men and women. Periodic attempts to clean up Dongguan through so-called Yellow Crackdowns were mostly ineffective. After one notable effort in February 2014, it was estimated that thousands of venues remained untouched.

I did not realize that I was observing first-hand the harsh conditions and struggles faced by many working-class migrant women who worked in the factories. I witnessed how sweatshops destroy hope and trap women in a downward spiral of despair. For these women, there are few options for a better life. That sex work consistently rescues them from the sweatshop should make people sit up and take notice. My connection protected me and provided me a private dormitory room. Usually blue-collar factory workers stay in a shared room. As I got to know people along the hall, I discovered that sweatshop workers typically live together six to eight to a room with little more than bunk beds and a single overhead fluorescent light. There was a strict lights-out policy at 10:00 pm, which was enforced by the factory. Ray said that this policy was common across the 20,000 factories in and around Dongguan. Very quickly I was able to learn how *dagongmeis* (factory girls) live.

From Farm to Sweatshop to Sex Work

During my third week of fieldwork, I met a young woman at the factory named Qiqi. Qiqi came from Sichuan province and was a typical 20-year-old with sparkling eyes and a wide smile, full of youthful optimism. At that point I had been collecting solid but not too surprising data about middle-class life in China, and as I walked past some women working on the assembly line, one of them suddenly looked up at me and boldly asked me who I was. In hindsight, I believe it took her some courage to approach me, a total stranger. Although I had tried hard to blend in, she and her friends knew that I was an outsider, a cosmopolitan stranger of higher status. To Qiqi and her friends, I was marked as an outsider by my Western brand-name clothing, which they made but could not afford to wear. Later I realized just how obviously my appearance and speech advertised that I was not one of them.

In our brief conversation that day, I explained to Qiqi that I was a doctoral student doing my fieldwork there. She was eager to hear about my past and the world I came from. Her questions about England and the United States revealed a sense of wonder about the world outside of China. Afterward she admitted that she longed for a better life, and thought perhaps one day she might be able to move to America. Qiqi had watched American TV shows where middle-class people lived lavish lifestyles, and she wished to become part of that cityscape.

Qiqi's personal charisma made her a leader of sorts among the women in the factory. She was outgoing and gregarious, a natural conversation-starter, and often the first to speak up about something. As it turned out, the others in that group had asked her to approach me first, to break the ice. Afterward, as we began to meet, the circle of connections opened up, and eventually I knew several women by name. Collectively they were quite careful not to reveal too much personal information about themselves until they were satisfied that I was not associated or affiliated with their boss.

Over the next several weeks, we hung out together and chatted countless times. Our conversations became more spontaneous and less guarded. Finally I felt it was appropriate for me to treat several girls at once to a group meal at a Western restaurant. At this café the set lunches ranged between 20 and 50 yuan (US$3–$8) per meal per person. To Qiqi and her friends, meals in cafés were a luxury and a special treat. They referred to it as "a city experience."

Whenever we were able to go to a new restaurant or café, I took the liberty of ordering for them so as to reduce the pressure of being in an unfamiliar environment. For example, the first time we went to Cowboy Café, Qiqi and her friends made a point of dressing up. They were visibly excited and studied the menu as soon as we sat down. The waiter greeted us and set down the complimentary glasses of water. As the girls sipped the water, exclamations of surprise abounded. Qiqi was incredulous as she exclaimed, "It has a lemon taste!"

These women were exploring a new world as they tried to navigate this foreign environment. They carefully asked me how to use the utensils, and which utensils went with which foods. They implored me to order for them as they were unsure even how to pronounce the name of the dish, much less what it would taste like. They were vulnerable and fearful of being exposed as country bumpkins in a "Western" space. Our group lunches were not frequent, since they worked 12-hour shifts pretty much every day with hardly any days off. The daily pressure to meet work quotas made it hard for these rural women to complain to their supervisors about the harsh working conditions.

Aside from taking them out for lunch, I also tried to visit them during their working hours. Every two hours each worker is allowed a short break to visit the restroom or grab a drink of water. During this time I could maintain relationships and even arrange to meet after the shift was over. One evening after her shift ended around 7:00 pm, Qiqi came to me clearly upset. With tears in her eyes, she said that this would be the last time I would see her. "I won't be here tomorrow, they are kicking all of us out," she said. "The news said the economy is going down and I guess we are going down first." She uttered a bitter laugh and wiped away her tears. As she started to walk away, she stopped and turned to me and quietly said, "They are firing so many of us." The resignation and hopelessness in her voice were heartbreaking. Soon afterward the factory closed and all the workers were let go.

From scattered conversations, I heard that many of them found new jobs; some settled down and got married. Others simply returned to their home province. They were all busy rearranging their lives, which were impacted by the global financial crisis. I, on the other hand, was busy conducting fieldwork and set about beginning to write my dissertation on the experiences of the new Chinese middle class. The last time I saw Qiqi at the factory was in August 2010.

Revisiting Dongguan in 2013

Three years later, when I finished my doctoral degree and came back to Dongguan in 2013, one of my friends from Hong Kong – I called him Henry – invited me to join him at a bar he owned. This low-end bar, called the Peach Bar, was located in a well-known entertainment area in Dongguan. All along the street, strings of bright festive lights tried to set a mood of revelry. Green, red, white, and blue posters adorned the street lamps, inviting (mostly) men to partake and relax. Everywhere I heard people laughing, chatting, and enjoying themselves. In the midst of this scene was the entrance to the Peach Bar. It was dimly lit with a soft red glow.

As we walked into the bar, Henry motioned towards the bartender and gave him a nod. We walked through a sliding door guarded by one man, and Henry politely introduced the area as the Peach Bar. As I entered, an overpowering wave of cigarette smoke and stale perfume enveloped me. Countless bottles of liquor had been drunk and spilled in this room. I discreetly rubbed my nose as I looked around with curiosity. There were probably as many as 150 women walking around in revealing tops and shorts and displaying long smooth legs in high heels. I turned to Henry, hoping he'd give me some answer as to who these women were. He smiled and remained silent as we walked towards a table. As we sat down, a woman came by and took our drink order while the soft plush sofa threatened to engulf me like quicksand.

A few minutes later, another young woman came towards us and placed the cocktails on our table. She sat down and strategically positioned herself facing Henry, with her back to me. I noticed that she lightly brushed his hand as she gave him his whisky on ice. Henry called over to me, "Her name is Rabbit and she comes from Sichuan." He chuckled and turned to her: "You do look like a rabbit! You are so

innocent and fair! You have the teeth too, and the cute round eyes."
Rabbit laughed demurely and then turned to greet me.

Suddenly we both froze. It was Qiqi! But this Qiqi was not the girl I
knew from the factory. She had sat down in character, but that façade
was now broken. I could only stare, and all she could say was, "I didn't
expect to see you here." Her discomfort at being found in a space like
this was obvious. I regained my composure and didn't say anything
overt because I wasn't sure how much she wanted to reveal in front of
Henry.

Afterwards, I learned that Henry had known that she was working in
the Peach Bar, and he also knew that Qiqi knew me. But he wanted to
surprise me and Qiqi. He was playing a practical joke on us. He smiled
and said, "Finally you guys meet in Peach Bar. Congratulations! Let's
celebrate with a champagne and enjoy your big reunion." Qiqi – the
innocent factory girl – was now Rabbit. Her skin now was glowing with
the help of bronzer. Her face had a peachy flush to highlight her youth,
and she sported short shorts that would have made her blush during
her factory days. She had transformed herself; in her words, she looked
"modern" (modeng 摩登).

After several rounds of drinks with various customers, Rabbit was
finally able to leave work and agreed that we could catch up over yexiao
(night snacks 夜宵). We left the club, and Qiqi went to her apartment
two streets over to change back to her "regular clothing." But her regular clothing now was nothing like what she had worn in the factory.
She wore skinny jeans paired with a sheer silk tank top, and she had
removed all her make-up except for a thin layer of sunscreen to cover
her dark freckled skin.

She was smiling as we walked side by side towards the restaurant of
our choice. We went to a noodle stand she liked on the side of the street,
and she said triumphantly, "Tonight, you can order anything you want
because now I have money." I told her that there was no need for her
to pay for my meal, but she insisted. We ordered two large bowls of
noodles and slurped away for a couple of minutes in silence. Finally, I
asked "So ... what happened? What are you doing now?" She stopped
slurping the noodles and thought for a moment before she told me her
story. "I got laid off and didn't have money to stay anywhere. I stayed at
my friend's house for a bit until she ran out of both money and patience,
then she kicked me out too. I tried so hard to look for a job, but you
know, I only graduated from primary school so no one wanted to hire
me. I worked in a bakery for a while but the pay was terrible. One
day I stole a bun to eat because I was so hungry. But I was caught and
got fired. After a month, I couldn't support myself anymore and my

tongxiang [fellow villager 同鄉] told me to go to this place. I had to go alone. I put on my best clothes and put on lipstick, so, you know, I could leave a good impression. The woman told me that I'd get at least 9,000 yuan [US$1,451] per month and maybe more with tips! I've never earned such a high salary and I didn't want to go home so ..." She then paused to sip her tea before telling me what she thought was the hardest part of the story.

"My family is poor. When I was 17 [2007] I had a son and he's with my parents. Now I need the money for him, you know. He's just a kid. I want to be able to get him a notebook for school. I want him to be able to graduate from high school because I never did. If I am able, I want to pay for him to go to university. I know this job is dirty and people look down on me. But if I can earn a lot of money then people will look at me differently." She defiantly thrust her arm towards me. "Look at this watch, a client gave it to me as a gift. It's a Michael Kors watch. Very expensive! People look at me differently now. Today I'm a city girl. Not a village girl. I didn't want to go home so I decided to do sex work because it's easier and it pays well. I am happy now that I chose sex work, now I'm sure I can afford my son's education and I can send money back to my parents for him. I even have spare money to spend on myself."

As she related her story I could only remain silent, poking around the leftover noodles in my bowl. She insisted that she was much happier now, and I could tell that she was more confident and in control. But I wasn't sure how much of that was just a façade. This was the moment when my research focus shifted. I was originally interested in exploring how migration and globalization restructured these migrant women's choices and lives. It now seemed that the next step in my research was to delve into the life choices of these women who argued and believed that sex work was a step up on their personal journey to success.

In the end, Qiqi decided to remain in the city as a commercial sex worker rather than return home to her rural village. She said: "If I stay here, I'm still a city girl. Actually I'm more of a city girl now. If I went back, my parents would just marry me off to someone so they could get some quick cash. But I want to be in control." Qiqi aspires to be an independent woman and she feels closer to that goal now than ever before. She makes fun of herself, the old Qiqi, who thought instant noodles were a luxury. Back then, she thought English was unfathomable and 600 yuan (US$90) was an unimaginable sum of money. Now, she is a cosmopolitan city girl who readily speaks English and routinely carries 600 yuan (US$90) in her purse. By her definition, she is a success.

To explore this further I enlisted the help of Kevin and Ken, who are the bosses of the mid-tier Lotus Club and high-tier Dragon Palace respectively, as well as Henry (the boss of the low-end Peach Bar). I approached each of them asking if I could work in each as a bartender to interview sex workers and clients.

This book explores the conditions where sex workers and their clients can generate intimate relationships that go beyond simple pecuniary transactions. Intimacy and reciprocating desire are rare, yet possible. Reciprocating desire refers to the dynamic interactions whereby clients remain attracted to the East Asian femininity constructed by the sex workers. It occurs most often in high-end bars among the high-end sex workers, but can happen anywhere. Forging a romantic or married rela- *leaving the work* tionship is a means by which some women can exit the commercial sex industry. Other high-end sex workers say that they gave up lucrative salaries and changed their career either through smart investing or launching their own business.

Masculinity is another focus in this book. The global financial crisis that emerged in 2008 shifted power relations and continues to redefine masculinity for both Western and Asian men in China. This book *entangled* extends Connell's hegemonic masculinity and proposes entangled mas- *masculinities* culinity. This concept includes different archetypes of masculinity and argues that masculinity is always multiple: a complex interplay of masculinities. Entanglement helps us understand how masculinities and desire are differentially articulated and shaped by external economic, institutional, and demographic changes as well as by heteronormative expectations. Entangled masculinities are tied to the post-socialist *post-socialist transition* transition that has reshaped China's social structure, economy, and culture. Specifically, we have the stories of single and young-adult male migrants who buy commercial sex from low-tier markets and streetwalkers and how they deal with the meaning of masculinity.

China's masculinity crisis is driven by economic and *hukou* (household registration) reforms. Policy changes enable and promote mass internal migration from inland China to coastal cities. A generation of the one-child policy has created a substantial gender imbalance in the young Chinese population. The resultant masculinity crisis expresses itself in tensions from which the single-adult migrants find it difficult to escape. These will be discussed in chapter 3.

The book situates the discussion of the "individualized self" within the context of the Chinese state. The Western individualized economy that emerged in China after the global financial crisis has been exacerbated by state-sanctioned capitalism and free trade. But the by-products are materialism and conspicuous consumption.

Encouraging this consumer revolution has come at the expense of political engagement during Xi's regime. This development is accelerating people's focus on feeding their individualized desires to climb the social hierarchy so they can enjoy cosmopolitan lives. This holds true not only for the average Chinese citizen but also for people on the fringe, such as sex workers, and especially sex workers from rural villages and farms. They quickly learn that when they have money, they can control their lives. The sex workers feel more cosmopolitan and individualized. They can even fulfil family obligations by financially supporting their parents back home in rural China. Therefore, the sex workers within the different niche markets are "bounded" by way of their position in the sociocultural context as an individualized self. Working in the sex industry not only improves their living conditions but also helps them pursue individualization which reflects the nation's transition to a country of individualized desires.

Overview of the Book

This book contains four parts and seven chapters. Chapter 1 provides the background and foundation for this ethnographic journey. It covers the inspiration, the methodological design, the qualitative perspective, and how ethnographic data was collected and analysed regarding the three niche markets in Dongguan. Chapters 2 and 3 focus on the plight of the low-end sex workers. Chapter 2 examines the life of the streetwalkers, as well as the low- and mid-tier bars where sex services are offered. Chapter 3 looks at the low- and mid-tier business from the perspective of clients; specifically, the single-adult migrant men who buy sex. This particular group has a number of conflicts regarding their masculinity and the expectations placed upon them by China's society. Together these chapters book-end the sociocultural space inhabited by the sex industry in China for low-end men and women.

Chapters 4 and 5 shift to the different worlds of opportunity that exist in high-end sex work, where money and connections lead to economic capital and the creation of intimacy. Chapter 4 examines how Chinese and foreign clients overcome social barriers to develop and consummate long-term relationships with sex workers. Chapter 5 looks at how high-end girls and their clients reciprocate sexual intimacy.

Chapters 6 and 7 focus on social policy implications and criminal justice. Chapter 6 presents the theoretical argument that selling sex is edgework for female sex workers. Edgework is voluntary risky activity that leads to new adaptive behaviours enabling the individual to continue that activity. The concept of edgework captures the perspective of a number of the women interviewed and offers a powerful explanation for why many will not leave. Chapter 7 closes the loop, bringing us back to the sweatshop factory life that many sex workers left in the first place. Once arrested, female sex workers (almost exclusively mid- and low-tier) and streetwalkers are sent to a custody education centre for "Re-education through Labour Camps" (RTLC) programs. These centres often fail at retraining because sex workers say they are humiliated, exploited, and abused. Perhaps worst of all, the labour actually mirrors that of the factory sweatshops. Finally, in the Conclusion, I summarize what we know about sex work in modern China and present my final insights, arguing for a fresh approach to urban sexscapes by rethinking intimacy, masculinity, and criminal justice in China's global commercial sex industry.

PART ONE

Method

Chapter One

Urban Sexscapes: A Snapshot of China's Commercial Sex Industries

The global economy of the 21st century is characterized by rapid social and economic change. The movement of vast amounts of wealth from the West to the East has brought extensive changes to the lives of 1.4 billion Chinese. The changing economics, coupled with the dynamic relationship between the transnational flow of capital and the highly localized urban geography of leisure, is altering the social and urban landscape. In the wake of these changes, China, and all of Asia, are evolving new ideologies about gender.

For women, the changes are complicated by clashes between traditional and modern social forces. Confucian traditions in China favour men and masculinity, as do the (often male-led) institutions guiding the nation today. But a decade of national economic prosperity is forcing individuals – both men and women – to re-evaluate their own definition of success. In every society there are winners and losers, predators and prey. In every boom, there are some who bust.

The commercial sex industry in China continues to flourish, and it is mostly managed by men, and men are the clients. The goodness or badness of commercial sex is best left to others; this book presents the stories and perspectives of women who had to make very difficult life decisions. All the women interviewed are pragmatic about their decisions and what they have cost.

Wherever there is money, power, and sex, there are entrepreneurs. There are some women who make sex work sound like a movie: beautiful people, lots of money, sensual fun and excitement. These are always the exceptions, the 1 per cent we see that covers up the 99 per cent we do not. Especially in the mid-tier or low-end bars as well as among streetwalkers, the story is much darker. Many women who worked in factories before the global financial crisis lost their jobs and jumped to the commercial sex industry. These women suffer from stigmatization and marginalization for being sex workers. When they are arrested for prostitution, they may be detained in custody education centres (Re-education through Labour Camps, or RTLC). These centres exist throughout China, and women I spoke with said that in them they experienced abuse, stigmatization, and exploitation. This book highlights the disparities between the official intentions of custody education and the day-to-day realities. Custody education is an ideal for rehabilitation that falls sadly short of its goals. The government must work harder so that this program does not become mere window dressing for a money-making enterprise. Complaints of internal corruption and human rights violations by local law enforcement officers must be taken seriously.

The Ethnography Approach

This book was based upon ethnographic field notes taken during two back-and-forth research excursions in Dongguan, South China. The first excursion was from September 2008 to December 2010, when I was still a doctoral student conducting my fieldwork, which at the time was to study the new Chinese middle class, particularly entrepreneurs who set up factories in Dongguan. Therefore, I had the chance to meet lots of female migrant factory workers. After my initial findings revealed that factory work was sort of a "gateway" to sex work, my focus shifted. The second excursion was from January 2013 to August 2017 and specifically targeted sex workers in China's commercial sex industry. Over those four-and-a-half years I conducted around 36 months of fieldwork, interviewing a total of 195 sex workers (targeting 50 from each niche market plus 45 streetwalkers).

This book uses pseudonyms for every interviewee. I find that the story "flows" better with names instead of markers or numbers. I am fluent in English and Chinese. However, some verbatim quotes may read a bit oddly because some Chinese expressions do not smoothly translate into English. I have tried to maintain the spirit and intention of what was said wherever I could. The book also adopted a longitudinal research method in following the sex workers, in order to know more about the changes they experienced in the commercial sex industry. I interviewed and followed 39 women who worked in the Dragon Palace and the Lotus Bar and who then married Hong Kong businessmen and moved to Hong Kong. The findings are presented in chapter 6. I also had the chance to interview 20 couples who are now living either in Hong Kong (6), London (4), Melbourne (4), Europe (3), or the US (3) by using telephone interviews during the summer of 2017. I originally met all of them in the Dragon Palace in 2013–17. Based on the longitudinal approach, I first re-contacted them via WeChat apps. Then I talked to them over the phone and examined how sex workers forged romantic relationships with their clients, married them, and then exited the commercial sex industry. The findings are presented in chapter 4.

Several male clients of sex workers were interviewed to bring much-needed perspective. Through my conversations – formal, informal, and group – I found approximately 200 clients who were willing to be interviewed: 30 local Chinese clients in each of low- and mid-tier bars ($30 \times 2 = 60$) and 50 in high-end bars, as well as 20 foreigners in each of low- and mid-tier bars ($20 \times 2 = 40$), a further 50 foreigners in high-end bars, as well as one owner of each bar. Five staff members were also interviewed.

My entrance into the world of bar eroticism was casual. To establish rapport with this hard-to-reach population, it was clear that I could not simply walk into the bar and fire off questions. The first week I simply prepared drinks and spoke with the girls and clients. Around the second week, girls began to open up and talk with me more. As I grew more familiar with the bar setting and the girls grew more familiar with me, I could approach them. In the Dragon Palace, Elsa and Vivian were the first two girls I told who I was and why I was there. In the Lotus Club, Wendy was the first one I met, and she helped me to settle in. In the Peach Bar, I knew Qiqi and Lotus when they worked in the factory, which made it easy for me to get into this bar. For streetwalkers, it wasn't until after our ice-breaking meeting that I discovered I had actually first met Dingding (24) when she worked in the factory, although neither of us remembered this at the time. With help from Dingding and Henry, it was easier for me to talk to the streetwalkers. For clients, I was more familiar with Mike (45) from the Dragon Palace, Dennis (40) from the Lotus Club, and Jiang (23) from the Peach Bar. The responses from sex workers and clients were guarded at first, but we kept talking. After that I could speak with other girls individually or in small groups. They then began to approach me discreetly when times were quiet or they were on break. By the fourth week I was able to collect data from in-depth interviews.

I knew up front that the bars appealed to different classes of clients. Money is a great divider even when the services are roughly the same. Upon reflection, the mid-tier was closer to the low-end bar in some respects, even though it charged closer to the average at the high-end. Men at the low-end bar might spend between 100 and 200 yuan (US$15–$30) for sex; at the mid-tier bar, the average charge was generally between 500 and 1,000 yuan (US$73–$145), and at the high-end bar the men seemed to cheerfully spend a minimum of 1,000 yuan (US$145).

Collecting Women's Stories: Ethnographic Journey and Methods

A conventional ethnographic-fieldwork approach was adopted, supplemented by less conventional methods such as "community talk," QQ/WeChat interviews, and photo-elicitation with the male migrants and female sex workers.

Fieldwork Entry

The importance of personal and professional networks cannot be stressed enough. As mentioned earlier, all names are pseudonyms. I was able to stay and work in the high-end bar in Dongguan, the Dragon Palace, because the owner, Ken, was someone I had known for many years from my days as an undergraduate student in Hong Kong. As my initial research began to shift from the factory to sex work, I spoke to a number of my old classmates for leads on bar owners in China. Ken's name came up, and I called him. When I asked him if he knew of any places in China involved with this type of activity, he simply invited me to look around his bar.

Henry, owner of the low-end Peach Bar, and Kevin, owner of the mid-tier Lotus Club, were also both former college classmates, so there was a degree of mutual trust which assured them that I was neither a police informant nor a crusader seeking to rescue them. In the same way, knowing these men from college (Henry and I had mutual friends) reassured me that I would be protected and watched over in this environment that was full of risk. In particular, Henry was a friend to many streetwalkers and played a vital role in putting me in contact with this very difficult-to-approach group. Henry was able to reassure both the bar girls and the streetwalkers that I was neither an undercover policewoman nor a spy. Kevin did the same for me at the Lotus Club.

Over the course of my research, I visited streetwalkers twice a week; the frequency of my visits enabled me to build rapport. The Peach Bar is a fixture located in the neon-soaked red-light district of Dongguan. Henry is well known and trusted by many of the streetwalkers, and he made the initial introductions and arrangements for them to talk to me. After they knew me, I could arrange to meet at nearby cafés and simply sit and chat with them. These field sites became familiar and easy for me to access through the development of these personal contacts and friendships. Inside the bars, I had to perform the role of bartender in order to "fit in." I learned those skills while in England working on my doctorate degree. I worked as a part-time bartender in a club in Birmingham for three years. In Dongguan I mostly poured beer, wine, and pre-made mixes, but in a pinch I could also make relatively simple combination drinks. This was enough to give me access to these clubs, and the owners could bring me in without calling too much attention to who I was and why I was there.

Afterwards, I could arrange the meetings on my own. Most often I would meet the girls individually at a nearby café. I gave cash coupons/non-cash gifts to all the informants who talked to me. Cash coupons valued at 200 yuan (US$30) were used as incentives to encourage the women and clients to participate in the in-depth interviews. Lunch or dinner was provided after the interview for those informants who could attend, and those who could not were given the coupons. The cash coupons were from the General Research Fund project of the University Grant Council in Hong Kong. While everyone had a different story and reasons for engaging in sex work, not one of them ever said they were forced into it. This is an important point because this research is not about the vicious and violent crime of human trafficking.

Because of the nature of this research, I worked as an unpaid bartender in the three bars for around 36 months of fieldwork over the summers from 2013 to 2017, much like other sex work ethnographers such as Zheng (2009) and Hoang (2015). A typical shift is twelve hours a day, seven days a week, during periods that last for three months. My working hours were quite flexible, and therefore I could talk to the sex workers and clients freely.

I did not rely entirely on in-person ethnography (Duneier, 2011). My fieldwork was supplemented by less conventional methods such as QQ/WeChat interviews. As it is difficult for informants to classify their own or others' behaviour, additional qualitative data was collected by photo-elicitation during the interviews and conversing with the clients and sex workers while walking around the sites (representing different niche markets). Inspired by Riessman (1993), I analysed the data in an ongoing, open-ended, and inductive way to ensure coherence, particularly global and thematic coherence. The client-worker relationship was explored through analysis of the respondents' personal accounts (global coherence). Next, prominent themes that emerged in these accounts were identified and analysed (thematic coherence). Inspired by Singer and Ryff (2001), I also used bottom-up analysis to explore each individual's personal account and then identified important commonalities and differences between accounts. The information collected during photo-elicitation and through the community walks was used to verify and amplify the data collected in the in-depth interviews. To carry out the photo-elicitation, I asked the informants to use their own photos, stored on their mobile phones or cameras, to help them describe their self-perceptions, cultural values, and worker-client relationships. The information obtained while walking with the informants around the bars supplemented and enriched the interview data.

Research Ethics

Data comprised recorded interviews, in situ note taking, and post-event field notes. Prior to any recorded interviews, all the interviewees signed consent forms, and my affiliated university granted me ethics approval. Before granting their consent, the respondents were given a copy of my business card and contact details. They were also reminded that they could freely withdraw without prejudice at any stage in the project. To safeguard the rights of the informants, I assured them that I was not an undercover policewoman and showed them my picture on my university staff identity card attached to a university-issued lanyard. The informants were fully assured at the outset of confidentiality and anonymity. For this reason, I only use their ages and assigned pseudonyms. All of the verbatim citations in this chapter were translated into English. I did not hide my identity as a researcher for this project. I did not ask for personal information such as official identification numbers or dates of birth.

Data Analysis

All the interviews were recorded, transcribed, and analysed by using a grounded theory approach and the software package Nvivo. The transcripts were analysed by using an analytic process to develop possible themes. I adopted an inductive analysis of the transcripts to see whether other themes or subthemes were possible. The dominant themes were "tempting girls" and edgework for the streetwalkers, and custody education for the low-end and mid-tier bar girls.[1] For the high-end bar girls and their clients, the major themes were intimacy, dealing with desires, changing career trajectories, marriage, and demonizing the "dirty girls'" identity. For the interaction between clients and sex workers, the theme of entangled masculinity will be identified, as will the way that men contracted their identities and masculinities. Transcripts were reread and validated against themes.

---

1 "Tempting girls" are different from factory girls (*dagongmei*). *Dagongmei* refers to female migrant workers or labourers. "Tempting girls" in this chapter refers to the former *dagongmei* who shifted to work in the sex industry after working as "factory girls." Strictly speaking, *dagongmei* is not equivalent to "tempting girls," since only some *dagongmei* become sex workers.

The Setting in Dongguan

In Dongguan, global and domestic financial wealth and rapid urban development have transformed the city into an increasingly cosmopolitan environment that has attracted many foreigners since China's accession to the World Trade Organization in December 2001. It is an important industrial city located in the Pearl River Delta and has over 25 million residents, accounting for a large portion of the population of Guangdong province. However, the city has an infamous reputation as a "sin city" and is home to many brothels, massage parlours, nightclubs, sex hotels, saunas, and karaoke bars.

Local authorities launched a Yellow Crackdown on the illegal sex industry in Dongguan on 9 February 2014. However, more than 3,000 entertainment venues in Guangdong suspected of involvement in the sex trade remained open (Davies, 2013). Furthermore, the Crackdown did not affect the high-end bars and hotels, whose owners had close "political" connections with the police and local government.

Dongguan was selected as the key field site because it has the greatest concentration of foreign nationals and capital in China. Besides the influx of low-income migrant communities, Dongguan also attracts a community of transient business professionals. This somewhat loose community is made up of upwardly mobile males who work for multinational and domestic corporations. The dominance of business activity and factory life in Dongguan meant that the 2008 global financial crisis had a significant impact on the city as vast numbers of migrant workers were made redundant by factories. Many migrant women found themselves newly unemployed in the city and unable to claim any benefits or social services; in effect, neither the private sector nor the social sector was able to provide any reliable forms of support.

Research Profiles

Streetwalkers

I met with the streetwalkers individually near the Peach Bar, and often spoke with them in a nearby café. Most of the streetwalkers I spoke with were aged from 20 to 50, and the mean age was 32 years. Their typical routine was to congregate along the back alleyways and side streets where the men knew to find them. The narrow back streets in China are dingy and dark. The girls have to stand along or lean against the dirty bricks in their tight garish blouses and too-tight, too-short skirts. The girls look like streetwalkers and that keeps things brutally honest.

There's very little chit-chat or flirting. The men walk up and simply ask, "How much?" and "Where?" There is nothing coy about the conversation. The men want sex, the woman are willing. The rest is haggling over price. It's a buyer's market conducted in the shadows and in the weak streetlight. Most of the women start working at first twilight and push themselves until dawn's first light, shortly after 5:00 am. Then it's home for a rest, to run some errands and start over again the next evening.

The women generally said that they received little or no education, and all admitted they came from rural areas. Of all the sex workers I interviewed, streetwalkers probably have the lowest self-image. They consider themselves less educated and less attractive than the sex workers who work in bars. Around half, 23 participants, had at least one child and were either still married or divorced. The other 22 participants were single.

All 45 sex workers interviewed were interprovincial migrants who came from Hunan, Hubei, Jilin, Sichuan, Anhui, or Hebei province and moved to Dongguan as *dagongmei*. Many of these women had either been laid off by employers or had willingly resigned from their previous jobs. Most of the women completed primary school; a quarter completed junior high; and one participant completed high school. Most of them had resided illegally in urban Guangdong for between one and three years, except for two women who had lived in Guangdong for more than ten years.

The overrepresentation among streetwalkers of women from within the sector of factory work reinforces some widely held stereotypes regarding the superior manual dexterity of young peasant women coupled with the practice of paying female workers less than their male counterparts (Jacka, 2009). Over 160 million rural women have migrated to the city since 1992, making up 33–50 per cent of China's rural migrant labour force (Chan, 2012). The mean monthly income for a streetwalker was 9,000 yuan (US$1,304). Obviously, in this uncontrolled environment, one would have difficulty in interviewing clients who buy sex on the street. However, based upon my participant observations, most of the clients come from among single and young-adult migrants, construction workers, blue-collar workers, and backpackers. They shared similar characteristics with the clients who were buying commercial sex in low-end bars.

A Low-End Bar: The Peach Bar

The low-end bar where I worked was called the Peach Bar. Located near the downtown area, the building itself was a garish, neon-soaked, single-story brick storefront, positioned between a convenience store and a small repair shop that closed at sundown. The bar was not ashamed of itself, blinking red neon and almost begging clients to take a chance there. The most comforting aspect of the bar was that its dishevelled appearance fitted the smell and the dirt and the shadows. Here it felt as if everyone had a price, and the price was low.

Near the Peach Bar, there were many streetwalkers either standing, smoking, talking on their phones, or chatting with other girls. Some lurked in the shadows and side streets; others seemed to meander aimlessly in a wide circle until someone approached them. Outside the main entrance of the bar was a small outdoor sitting area, much like an outdoor café. A couple of small plastic tables with a few plastic chairs were positioned under a portable umbrella, presumably for the clientele to enjoy the stale night air. Inside, there was a long bar across from a stage, and tables and chairs to seat around 50–75 customers. Down the hallway were a few small private rooms. Inside the bar, there was a concourse and a stage. The boss's office was on the other side of the bar near the entrance and next to the restrooms. During my research, the Peach Bar underwent remodelling and decoration; in a touch of irony, the proprietors used large posters of Mao Zedong as a public façade to hide the nature of the business.

Under the Yellow Crackdowns, many girls have found creative and resourceful ways to survive. For them it is easier to earn money in Hong Kong because they do not need to work with police or organized crime figures. Still, many girls must work and travel from city to city, living a transient, "hard to find" life. Additionally, many have started to rely upon QQ, Weibo, or Renren (social media platforms) to find and maintain contact with clients. They also use the online platforms to recruit other workers, but they must be very careful and discreet. The transactional WeChat or Weibo uses a members-only arrangement, so one can only gain access if referred or verified by an existing client. It is crucial for the clients to pay the membership fee up front to gain access into the WeChat or Weibo group. These chat groups are critical for women to find work.

SEX WORKERS AT THE PEACH BAR

Many of the sex workers at the Peach Bar were older, less attractive, and/or less educated than those at the higher levels. They survived in this environment by doing whatever they could to attract customers and get as much money as possible. Most of the low-end sex workers in the Peach Bar were aged from 18 to 50, and the mean age was 36. Most of them came from rural China with little to no economic resources or social networks that might enable them to use technologies of embodiment, such as plastic surgery for a nose job or breast enlargements

(Hoang, 2010, 2011, 2014a). They tended to experience higher rates of police harassment, sexual abuse, and sexually transmitted diseases.

Many of the girls I met there had actually worked in the factory I visited in my previous field research work. They had all lost their jobs when the factory closed down in the wake of the 2008 global financial crisis. Scrambling for income, many of these girls ended up working at the Peach Bar. They also engaged in some very risky practices. For example, since "virgins" get the highest price, I learned that it was not unusual for some of them to use animal blood on a sponge, inserted just before intercourse. I met one woman who had performed this deception three times.

The sex workers at these centres are depressingly pragmatic. They have no interest in flirting or fantasy and mechanically engage only in sex-for-cash exchanges. In addition, Peach Bar sex workers have to bribe the police and the triads (gangs) for their own safety because sex work is illegal and therefore somewhat dangerous. The Peach Bar women are on QQ lists advertising female companionship, which allows local Guangdong men or drivers from Hong Kong or Macau to find them. In the club, the women routinely perform stripteases on stage as a way to drum up business. Afterwards, they privately arrange for additional services with interested customers.

Migrant sex workers cannot escape their fate. They never wanted to be used by men as sexual playthings and toys. The girls in the Peach Bar might be able to satisfy their materialistic goals, but the dream to "make good, be good" soon evaporates when they fail to find marital partners or otherwise cannot have traditional families. Sex workers are in need of help and education, to press for rights and benefits. They are very conscious of their powerlessness in Chinese society, and many have no means to further their own interests. This is where non-government organizations, guilds, or even the government can intervene.

CLIENTS AT THE PEACH BAR
The men who frequented the Peach Bar came from diverse backgrounds, yet were typically low-income earners, like the clients of the streetwalkers: migrant workers, construction workers, Hong Kong truck drivers, or backpackers, mainly from North America and Europe. Most of the backpackers were English teachers in Guangdong province. The local Chinese came from interprovincial migration, primarily from Hunan, Hubei, Jilin, Sichuan, Anhui, and Hebei provinces; most were born in rural communities. Among 50 clients, the ages for the clients ranged from 29 to 45 and the mean age was 32. On average, most of the men reportedly spent 150–300 yuan (US$22– $45) on various sexual services such as oral, anal, penetrative, and vaginal sex. Understandably, the relational ties between the workers and clients were typically weak.

A Mid-Tier Bar: The Lotus Club

The mid-tier bar I attended was called the Lotus Club and mainly catered to middle-class Chinese and foreigners. The Lotus Club was located in a better part of town, and the street was noticeably cleaner than that of the Peach Bar. There was no neon or red light, but the front was decorated and brightly lit. Inside the furnishings were nicer and cleaner than those in the Peach Bar. This club was actually smaller than the Peach Bar but extended upward three stories.

The first floor was the familiar bar-across-from-a-stage, but the stage was rarely used and the table seating accommodated fewer than 30 customers. This space was mostly for clients to wait or engage in chit-chat with the girls afterwards. Off to the side of the bar was a foyer where the madam welcomed clients and could bring girls to them for inspection. Behind a large Yin-Yang poster at the back of the club was a hidden exit that patrons could use in the event of a police raid. The exit led down a dim, narrow hallway to a plain metal door. Pushing past the self-locking door, you found yourself suddenly standing in a crowded residential market area, a safe distance from the main entrance.

The second floor was entirely reserved for the owner. It had offices and a private room for entertaining. Above that, on the third floor, there were a dozen rooms, each with a private bathroom, bed, and amenities like mood lighting, wall decorations, and curtains on the windows.

SEX WORKERS AT THE LOTUS CLUB

Many of the girls working here were relatively young, between the ages of 20 and 28, with a mean age around 25. Most of them had graduated from junior secondary school and worked in a factory before they entered the sex industry. Many of these women told me that they had been married and had left children behind in their hometowns in North China, in the care of husbands and/or parents. There was some similarity between mid-tier and high-end bar girls regarding emotional labour, as some girls could move to the high-tier bars. These girls were young and had more body/erotic capital and emotional strength. Besides the sexual services performed in private, these women provided added benefits through more "relational" behaviours like humour, chit-chat, active listening, and even cooking or non-sexual massage. Girls in the Lotus Club strove to be more than sex objects or toys, and instead worked to construct visible power relations between them and the client. Through interpersonal communication strategies, these women created an illusion of dependency and sought sympathy or compassion. They capitalized on it and used it as a way to signal for repeated and regular interactions, resulting in more financial support. When they were downstairs in the public bar area, the women demurely poured beer, caressed customers' arms or shoulders, and flirted with their eyes. Their standard attire was tight skinny jeans and short shirts, bright make-up and fashionable jewellery. They helped their clients feel attractive and powerful in the public sphere.

CLIENTS AT THE LOTUS CLUB

This bar catered mostly to middle-class Chinese and foreigners. Among the foreign respondents, many were from developed Western countries and had come to China to "seek adventure" and start a new life after the global financial crisis. The middle-class Chinese men either came from Hong Kong or overseas from North America or Europe. The 50 clients I interviewed were aged between 25 and 50, and the mean age was 36. The membership arrangements allowed overseas Chinese to jump the queue, find tables quickly, and sit with the prettiest sex workers available. The quality and performance of sex workers not only reflected male clients' economic power but conveyed class privilege and helped clients to expand their networks and business. Most of the Chinese middle-class clients I observed and could speak with had been living abroad, but had returned to take advantage of China's growing economy.

A High-End Bar: The Dragon Palace

The Dragon Palace was a well-known "gentlemen's club" and five-star hotel located in a respected commercial centre of Dongguan. It was surrounded by other reputable restaurants and bars which were very popular at night. The Dragon Palace entrance was guarded by a smiling concierge who would politely ask if you had a membership. Admission to the Dragon Palace was by membership or invitation only from either an affiliated sex worker or the bar owner. The club occupied seven floors and was an impressive combination of glass, steel, and light. The walls were bedecked in gold and yellow, which complemented the opulent feel conveyed by the royal décor. The design was notably European; the concourse was breathtaking in its splendour. The ceiling was high and decorated throughout with images from Greek mythology, but also Christian iconography such as angels and cherubs. Inside, the furnishings were lavish and well kept. There were rooms and facilities for every type of activity. The main club area seated around 200 and provided a full dining menu and bar, complete with attendants and waitstaff. It looked rich and successful and expected its clients to be the same.

In total there seemed to be around 200 female sex workers in this bar when I worked there. The female restroom was kind of a social area, and often one could find women there singing, practising pole-dancing moves, gossiping, laughing, watching movies on their smartphones, reading fashion magazines, or polishing their finger-nails. Some just quietly sat and smoked cigarettes. A few would even have a drink. The Dragon Palace provides "anti-raid" training ses-sions. The girls were trained to dress quickly – within 30 seconds – after a warning siren sounded. They left the scene using a designated safe passageway. The bar also arranged for a native English speaker to regularly help the women improve their English. Most of these sex workers read online newspapers daily on their smartphones. They also watched news on television, listened to the radio, and read magazines to keep up to date on current affairs. Most of the sex workers were free to leave after their shifts and often went to hang out with friends or clients in hotels, homes, or some resort areas outside Dongguan.

The bar owner charged 40 per cent of the total cost of the services from the sex workers. The sex workers could keep 60 per cent profit for each ser-vice from their clients. There were on average perhaps 200–400 customers per night, maybe more during weekends or public holidays. The Chinese and non-Chinese clients seldom interacted except when they indulged in bragging or showing off their wealth by giving large tips. Any hint of physical violence was strictly prohibited as the boss wouldn't allow fights and violence to destroy the reputation of the bar. However, clients would compete for the services of the same bar girls. Clients often showed off by purchasing expensive champagne (like Dom Perignon) or whisky. If the client ordered enough bottles of expensive champagne, the sex worker would deliver a tub of sparklers or even small fireworks to the table. This allowed everyone in the bar to know who was racking up the most expen-sive bill for the night. The surreal environment was a fascinating look into the lives of sex workers and clients as I made drinks for customers.

SEX WORKERS AT THE DRAGON PALACE

Most of the women who worked in this bar graduated or at least attended college. They were clearly more educated than the girls in the low-end bars. These women were young "professional cuties," aged 18 to 25, with an average age around 22 years. They all graduated from secondary school or post-secondary school and were able to carry on simple conversations in English. Many of these girls also came from relatively well-to-do families and had the economic resources necessary to maximize their physical assets through technologies of embodiment. These procedures are expensive and often involve travel to Korea or Thailand. Further, these women tended not to be the sole breadwinners for their family, unlike some migrant workers, which provided them a degree of financial freedom. They still faced greater economic challenges than their parents, yet did not look to collective forms of support for their financial future. In their view, they could choose their own job and determine their life chances.

The sex workers in the Dragon Palace said that they rarely experienced police harassment and reported lower rates of sexually transmitted disease or sexual abuse. Like their counterparts in the Lotus Club, their standard daily attire appeared to be tight jean shorts, shaved legs, fashionable jewellery, and bright make-up. Higher earnings enabled them to immerse themselves in global consumer culture, providing them not only material resources but also the chance to improve their self-worth and social standing.

CLIENTS IN THE DRAGON PALACE
This bar catered to wealthy Chinese men and wealthy foreigners. At the Dragon Palace the minimum charge for sex was 1,000 yuan (US$150), and the maximum charge was euphemistically said to be "whatever the market (the client) can bear." These men were part of an elite membership network that provided them exclusive entry to the bar and the opportunity to reserve a VIP room (baofang 包房). Among 80 clients (30 Chinese, 50 foreigners) I met at the Dragon Palace, most were wealthier and better connected in Dongguan than those at the other bars. Most of them were aged 22–50, and the mean age was around 34. The women who worked at Dragon Palace were part of contemporary China's contingent of high-end sex workers. As such, these women were expected to understand the nuances of the business interactions and communications that occurred at the club. These women must know when to speak, when to be silent, when to leave a room, and when (and how) to best attend to the clients' wishes.

Conclusion

This book was based on interviews conducted with many sex workers and clients in Dongguan. Sex work is illegal in China, and it is important to develop trust through personal connections. By spending time with these women (and men), I was able to gain valuable insights into how the commercial sex industry operates in China. I also saw that it is a bit different from the horror stories of human trafficking and slavery that reflect what goes on in so many other parts of the world. This is not to say these things do not happen in China, but the time I spent witnessing interactions, pickups, and hookups, I saw that for many of those involved, sex work was a way to get sexual satisfaction for a price as everyone tried to make it through another day of a difficult life.

PART TWO

"Tempting Girls" and Clients in Low-End and Mid-Tier Niche Markets

Finding Hope as a "Tempting Girl" in China: Sex Work, Indentured Mobility, and Cosmopolitan Individualism

I remember the first day I met Dingding as a streetwalker. I asked my friend Henry to get me in touch with one, and he knew several street-walkers through his Peach Bar. Henry gave me Dingding's contact information, and I briefly spoke with her over the phone. She agreed that I could visit her at her home address. It was walking distance from the club, and I set out on foot around mid-day to find her. Some 20 minutes later, as I turned the last corner before her address, I came upon a 20-something-year-old woman smiling broadly and talking to a young man just out of his teens. They were standing at her door and I caught the tail end of the conversation. "Do you want to try some exciting experience with my devil hands for only 250 yuan [US$40]? Do you want to try it little brother?" Her voice was a sultry mix, gentle yet full of titillation. He went inside and less than half an hour later the door opened and the young man quickly walked away. Now, it was just the two of us. She silently studied me with steely eyes. I was wearing a long-sleeved buttoned-up dress shirt, dress pants, and Oxford shoes, marking me clearly as neither a sex worker nor a client. A frown suggested that she was puzzled as to why I was there. Finally she spoke, loud enough for anyone to hear: "Who are you? Why are you here?" From our earlier phone call, I recognized the voice of Dingding with her strong Beijing accent (*jingpianzi* 京片子).

She was not comfortable around me at the beginning. As I tried to explain who I was and why my research was important, she kept herself in constant motion. She fidgeted and rearranged things, avoiding all eye contact with me. I kept on, trying to win her confidence, imploring her, and reassuring her about the significance of the information I wanted her to give me. Several times I thanked her for her time and for granting me this opportunity to speak with her. Still, she did not directly respond to me. As she put on her make-up and clothes for her shift that afternoon, I thought I had lost.

Finally, she picked up her cigarettes and asked if I minded if she smoked. I tried one last gamble and said, "No, it's okay. I smoke too." She offered me a cigarette, and at that moment, the wall came down. Finally, it seemed, we had something in common, a "bad habit" that could now tie us together. As she moved closer to light my cigarette, I could tell that she was starting to let her guard down. She slowly exhaled smoke and started speaking with me. She said in an even tone, "I am going to tell you what I have experienced as a streetwalker. More stories will come since you are Henry's friend. I trust Henry, but not you ..." I was shocked by her honesty, but in China this is understandable. I was on my way, but I had far to go to win her trust.

Dingding comes from Fujian, a coastal province about seven hours' drive north of Guangdong. She moved to Dongguan when she was 19 and worked in a factory there for five years. She left the factory and plunged into life as a low-end sex worker in the Peach Bar in 2010. She wanted more flexible hours and left the Peach Bar to become a streetwalker, which she has been since 2013. Dingding said that she has to dress seductively. Standard attire is low-cut tight dresses that barely cover her hips and breasts, or short shorts and sheer blouses that leave little to the imagination. Out on the street, she has to approach potential clients and try to lure them with flirting and sweet come-ons. Her main work area is the public park near the Peach Bar. Her striking eyes glow under Dongguan's neon lights, capturing the attention of construction workers, factory workers, and businessmen from Hong Kong. Dingding is a little bit different from the other streetwalkers I met. She only has a primary school education but shows incredible savvy and "street smarts."

Dingding told me that she wrote a poem in Chinese:

起床、上班,
工作、下班,
非人生化及身體像機器樣被肢解的生活,
為生計所迫,
身體隨着痛苦的節奏律動,
大聲呼喊卻無人回應,
我還能做甚麼?

Here is the translation:

To get up, to work,
To be on duty, to get off duty,

Dehumanized and mechanical dismemberment,
Work hard to make a living,
Body rhythm by torturous beats,
We shouted loudly but nobody helps,
What can I do?

However, if she could choose it again, she would still be a street-walker and work in Dongguan's commercial sex industry. She said,

Am I ashamed of being a sex worker? Who cares? Money is king ... I am happy that I can make this choice.

(Dingding, 24)

Like many of the women I interviewed from 2008 to 2010, Dingding migrated to the city as one of contemporary China's growing contingent of working girls. These women, referred to as "tempting girls," became streetwalkers after working as "factory girls." These "tempting girls" are a subset of a larger group of rural-to-urban migrants that character-izes the social and economic landscape of contemporary China. That so many of these peasant girls end up in China's urban commercial sex market is a significant social issue. This chapter examines how migrant workers become sex workers within the academic discussion of agency in sex work. The transition from factory sweatshop to sex work not only is a form of indentured mobility but also reflects a bounded rational choice. Why do streetwalkers continue to work even after they have earned more than enough from prostitution to quit? Why do they treat it as a long-term "career" when they claim that they initially got into it as a short-term or temporary move? Money is a factor, but these streetwalkers say that they are pursuing something more meaningful. Despite the deplorable and harsh conditions, these women still prefer sex work to the factory. They have made a deliberate choice to engage in sex work as a means of embracing individualism and cosmopolitanism, which will enhance their future livelihoods.

As is clear from Dingding's experience, the factory environment marginalizes young, undereducated migrant women, forcing them to reconsider their aspirations and motivations with respect to their rural-urban migratory journey. The end result is their choice to engage in sex work. While Parreñas (2011a) highlighted how contractual stipulations and working under pimps constricted women working as hostesses, at least some streetwalkers seem to enjoy a more individualized self.

Dingding laboured under gruelling conditions in a garment factory for five years before making the transition to streetwalker. Her path, from rural farm to urban factory to become one of Dongguan's street-walkers, is not unusual. Rather, Dingding's trajectory into sex work reflects the bounded rational choice that many former *dagongmei* make when leaving factories for employment in the commercial sex industry. Sex workers report a better income, greater personal freedom, and less exhausting labour conditions.

The streetwalkers I interviewed were keenly aware of their vulnerable situation. Providing sex to clients (mainly working-class Chinese) on the street is full of risks. There are the occupational hazards of dealing with pimps and gangsters on the one hand and avoiding the police on the other. Physical violence is as likely as arrest, and sexual harassment is routine from all sides. There are also health risks from sexually transmitted diseases such as HIV/AIDS.

Another streetwalker I met was Xiaoxiao. She was a sex worker at the Peach Bar in 2010 and later left to become a streetwalker. Smoking a cigarette in tight skinny jeans, bright make-up, and flashy jewellery, she responded candidly when I asked if she had any regrets about becoming a sex worker:

> Even if the factory I worked in before didn't close, I'd still have chosen to be a prostitute. Can you imagine that I had to sew more than 120 pairs of jeans per hour? It is crazy to sew 120 pairs of jeans per hour ... China is in a consumer revolution, everyone wants to shop, and it is too bad if you are without money. At that time, I only considered money and didn't want to remain working in that factory like a slave. I want a happy and comfortable life, and be able to decide my own life ... I am the breadwinner in my family.
>
> (Xiaoxiao, 20)

Streetwalkers exemplify what is referred to as indentured mobility. Although they work under pimps and must hide their occupation from family and friends, they still prefer working in the commercial sex industry. All the informants in this chapter asserted that being on the street was better than being in the factory.

From Factory to Sex Work: The Context

These migrant working women typically began their urban sojourns working in sweatshop factories before segueing to sex work. More than 70 per cent of my informants were born after 1980 and are second-generation migrant workers with fewer obligatory economic burdens than the first generation. They are characterized by their drive for a better quality of life, which is due to their knowledge of urban life. Furthermore, they enjoy a better governmental infrastructure that has protected workers' rights since the labour shortage of 2004 (Choi & Peng, 2015). However, prospects for unskilled migrant workers remain bleak. Conditions have deteriorated since the global financial crisis of 2008–9, when around 200,000 *dagongmei* were fired with almost no notice (Phillips, 2013). Even today, women in low-paying factory jobs face a bleak economic outlook, exacerbated by diminishing global demand for designer clothing. Many factory workers must work an astounding 360 hours per month, which equates to 12 hours per day every day without rest.

The disappointment with city life is compounded by meagre salaries and uncertain pay. According to Lee and Shen (2009, p. 120), only 48 per cent of workers in garment factories received their wages on time, and an estimated 54 per cent were forced to work without either basic salaries or overtime pay. Therefore, the decision to leave the factory for sex work is simple mathematics. Factory work pays an average monthly earning of 1,600 yuan (US$235) while sex workers report an average monthly income of 8,000–10,000 yuan (US$1,176– $1,470).

The *Hukou* System

Dagongmei differ from their better-educated rural counterparts who are employed in the city's informal service sector. The ubiquity of rural migrants with urban aspirations raises several questions regarding the social future of the migrant sex workers who are interwoven into the fabric of China's burgeoning metropolises. Peasant-migrant workers participating in urban sex work are not entitled to *hukou* or household registrations in the city (Mallee, 2003). *Hukou*, put simply, is a government-instituted household registration system prohibiting rural citizens from residing permanently in urban areas without state approval. The system was conceived to bind citizens to their birthplaces, ensuring that individuals would be dependent upon their specific rural or urban collectives for employment and subsistence. However, the contemporary labour demands within China require much of the rural populace to migrate to urban areas. As a consequence, the *hukou* system disadvantages the rural poor who do not qualify for the privileges and rights accorded to individuals with the urban *hukou*. In fact, upon commencing employment in Guangdong, *dagongmei's* precarious lifestyles are comparable to those of illegal aliens residing in a foreign country who lack the right of permanent abode. For this reason, *hukou* has been criticized as a uniquely Chinese state apparatus that spatializes inequality.

Without urban registration, illegal rural workers in metropolitan China are ineligible for state insurance or welfare benefits.

Each of the sex workers I interviewed unanimously hates the *hukou* system, because if they get sick in the city they must return to their home-town for treatment (Kong, 2016) or pay extra for local care. These women are denied access to public services, basic welfare, health care, and afford-able public housing in urban China. Migrant women are marginalized and face a high rate of labour abuse, a culture of widespread prejudicial attitudes towards them, and socio-economic disparities between urban and rural communities (Kong, 2016). In the particular context of the 45 women I interviewed who were *dagongmei*, their prospects were point-edly bleak. Additionally, their labour conditions included daily expe-riences of flagrant sexual harassment, exhausting working conditions, and labour violations. Many of the women affirmed that prostitution actually seemed a step up from working in the factory.

Conceptualizing the Choice and Force Debate

There are diverse perspectives on female migrant workers becoming sex workers, including pull-push factors (Ravenstein, 1885; Lee, 1966), psychological motivations (James & Meyerding, 1977; Miller, 1986), and financial factors (Brown, 1978; Miller, 1986; James & Meyerding, 1977; Laner, 1974). Other scholars (Klinger, 2003) focus on the role of agency to explain why sex workers enter the industry and then leave after earning enough money. By and large, this literature sees *choice* as the key. This scholarship argues that sex workers make independent and informed decisions about using their bodies and sexual skills for their own ends. Researchers found some women engage in sex work just long enough to make quick cash for immediate personal or family-related reasons (Zheng, 2009; Otis, 2011; Liu, 2012). Other researchers report that many sex workers in China are forced into the business and do not work for their own personal benefit (Zheng, 2009). Women face numerous double standards involving moral and social codes, such as maintaining family honour via their own chasteness and meeting filial financial obligations.

Navigating the physical environment is the greatest struggle. Sex workers are in constant danger of sexual violence, police beatings, and a variety of verbal abuse. The literature on Chinese women who were sex workers fails to acknowledge that a substantial number participate in commercial sex work because it is the "least worst" of several poor options. For example, Fangfang (20) described one abusive encounter. She said her typical asking price for sex was approximately 65 yuan

(US$10). However, one client (a local old Chinese man) refused to use a condom and suddenly pushed her to her knees. He grabbed her head and forcibly raped her mouth until he ejaculated. Then he refused to pay, mocking her and claiming that they had agreed on vaginal sex and not oral sex. Fangfang was under a lot of financial pressure at the time, so she could only watch him leave. Despite her humiliation, she had to pick herself up and go on to try to find her next client. Huiling (20) – whom I met in a dilapidated, dimly lit hotel room – sneered at the thought of developing intimacy with a client. She is always worried that she will contract a contagious disease like AIDS from customers. Despite this and constant police harassment, she still insists she wants to remain a streetwalker.

At present there is a well-established literature on rural-to-urban migration in post-socialist China which investigates migrants' subjectivities, hardship, agency, and experiences under the state's structural constraints (Fan, 2008; Jacka, 2009; Lee, 1998; Pun, 2005, 2016; Zheng, 2009) in a factory regime. Many studies also focus on the Chinese regulatory structure as an underlying factor to explain why migrant workers become sex workers. Zheng (2009) suggested that the Chinese state was complicit in expanding the sex industry and thus contributed to the exploitation of sex workers. Choi (2011) noted the Chinese state's repressive measures against prostitution. Sex workers were portrayed in the national discourse as victimizers spreading disease and hampering efforts to promote safe sex (Choi & Holyroyd, 2007; Pan, 1999, 2000). The arguments against legalizing sex work are largely driven by the stigma attached to it and the refusal to recognize female body autonomy. This narrow focus on sex workers as victims ignores the possibility of an individualized self (Bernstein, 2007; Brennan, 2004).

There is little published literature on the contractual stipulations of sex work. Women must work with pimps and gangsters while avoiding police, yet they still remain committed to their jobs and even imply that they're satisfied with their individualized self (Rosen & Venkatesh, 2008; Tsang, 2017b). The individualized self here means that the streetwalkers have autonomy and freedom to choose their own lives.

Beck and Ritter (1992) suggested a categorical shift in the relationship between the individual and society. That is, the self-radicalization of modernity has set the individual free from most of the previous all-encompassing social categories in industrial society, such as family, kinship, gender, and class, and the individual has emerged as the reproduction unit for the social in a risk society. Beck and Ritter's individualization thesis is appropriate in understanding the Chinese case because it focuses on the structural changes in the individual-society-state relationship instead of on any political philosophy or ideological imperative. Also, there is a dearth of literature on why sex workers, having met their immediate financial needs, choose to stay in the commercial sex industry. To this end, I want to probe the relationship between sex work and the concepts of indentured mobility and bounded rational choice.

Indentured Mobility   *Lipstick capitalism*

Indentured mobility identifies the "process of migration as producing economic mobility at the cost of the migrant becoming an unfree laborer" (Parreñas, 2011a, p. 328). By "unfree laborer," Parreñas, whose fieldwork was in Japan, refers to how these women lack control over their labour and are often not compensated until the end of their contracts. They are financially beholden to various middlemen who facilitate their travel and employment upon arrival in Japan (Parreñas, 2011a).

BOUNDED RATIONAL CHOICE

In contrast to indentured mobility, the notion of bounded rational choice explores the options that exist for sex workers within the context of the conditions they face. Rosen and Venkatesh (2008) found that bounded rationality has explanatory power for low-end sex workers in Chicago. The bounded rationality argued by Simon (1955, 1956) explains similar decisions by the streetwalkers in Dongguan. It is not feasible for human beings to make perfectly rational decisions when faced with limited information on options; instead they opt for satisfactory and comfortable ones. In both cities, sex work provides autonomy and personal fulfilment, even as it mitigates the consequences of poverty and income instability. The interpersonal, structural, and economic circumstances that low-income individuals navigate make those options that are available in the formal labour market appear to be undesirable and even unacceptable (Jeffrey & MacDonald, 2006, p. 322).

cf Bourgois

Indentured Mobility and Bounded Rational Choice for Streetwalkers in China

The streetwalkers I interviewed carefully weighed their options regarding money, independence, and flexibility. Staying in the commercial sex industry became a feasible, if not preferred, alternative. Likewise, the streetwalkers in my research overwhelmingly preferred sex work to low-wage sweatshop work. They made this choice despite being subjected to formal contractual or professional agreements with pimps. Conversely, they were "bounded" by way of their position in the sociocultural context as an individualized self. Bounded rational choice is part of a process that is calculated and rational and carefully evaluated by the individual, who is, in turn, bound to the sociocultural context of China as a cosmopolitan and individualized self.

Streetwalkers in Dongguan also enjoy certain financial freedoms and hope for upward mobility (Craig & Fournet, 1987; Goldstein, 1982); these low-educated migrant women are fighting to survive in highly competitive urban environments. They are faced with limited choices within both the formal and informal labour markets. The streetwalkers interviewed all regularly deal with bribes, the threat of arrest, and various forms of harassment, yet they want to stay in the sex industry. However, Parreñas's (2011a) indentured mobility focuses more on the contractual agreements signed with the middleman while neglecting the individualized self as a bounded rational choice. In effect, bounded rational choice highlights the fact that women are "bounded" by circumstances, internal motivations, and external structures. It is a carefully considered deliberate choice to control their lives.

From Retrenchment to Sex Work: A Mobility of Choice

As relevant literature and interview testimonials reveal, the gruelling and harsh demands of factory labour were a critical factor driving these women to explore an alternative career as a sex worker. The decision to choose sex work over factory migrant work stems from indentured mobility to enjoy freedom, autonomy, and flexibility in the commercial sex industries.

Factory Life

Meifang, a streetwalker who previously worked in a factory, elaborated on the dismal working conditions and unrealistic demands that led her to pursue sex work. She said,

> We were required to sign a contract stating that we wouldn't go to the toilet more than three times per working day and that we wouldn't spend more than 10 minutes during each visit, the consequences would be severe if we breached these requirements.
>
> (Meifang, 23)

In addition to the insights provided by the participants, relevant literature similarly highlights extensive workplace injustices and abuses. The harsh realities of the factory are exacerbated by the fact that many of these "tempting girls" are not prepared to enter these working environments. Several interviewees said that they were initially optimistic about factory work because the factories provided an opportunity to gain experience in the city as well as to meet potential partners while earning a waged income. However, their experiences revealed that the formal labour market often failed to provide a healthy and safe environment for its workers. As a consequence, these women, who travelled to Dongguan seeking a stable income, were offered limited job options and their rights as workers were not respected.

Although the harsh and jarring conditions of factory life are not the sole determining factor in the transition to sex work, the women interviewed said they never considered sex work before they entered the factory. This is not to suggest that the women were wholly ignorant of Dongguan's sex industry. In fact, many participants were highly aware of Dongguan's reputation and heard stories of women who were able to achieve upward mobility through sex work. However, the women interviewed said their decisions to leave their hometowns were based primarily on getting a good job in the city. Sex work only became an alternative once they encountered factory life and had to look for ways out.

Remuneration

Although harsh labour conditions were discussed extensively, the issue of money was the primary and most critical factor motivating women to enter sex work. This aspect is typical within similar economic contexts wherein low-wage manual labour is an integral component of the economy and culture of bourgeoning urban centres (Jacka, 2009, p. 277; Busza, 2004). In my sample, factory work yielded an average monthly earning far below what could be earned in the commercial sex industry.

Yuemiao highlights the role of remuneration in her decision to leave the factory and pursue sex work. She notes:

> I remember the average monthly salary was around 1,600 yuan [US$232]. This includes the entire basic salary and overtime pay. I worked a total of 390 hours a month, working a 30-day month and an average of 13 hours a day. The monthly salary statement for an ordinary worker would be around 1,000 yuan [US$145] for basic pay, merit pay at 50 yuan [US$7.50]; full attendance bonus at 40 yuan [US$6 for two holidays a month]; an overtime pay at a rate of five yuan [less than US$1] per hour. The combined overtime pay can be as much as 300 yuan [US$43] or more per month for those who work a total of 100 hours at night per month. When I fell sick and asked for leave, they deducted my salary.
>
> (Yuemiao, 23)

In the factory, we would be penalized if we left for lunch and would have our salaries deducted. I was forced to work overtime even though I could prove that I suffer from health problems. They would still deduct my salary. If I refuse to work overtime, I'd be threatened with dismissal. I even had to sign a form declaring that I wouldn't hurt myself at work and that my family wouldn't be paid compensation in the event of any injuries sustained, not even in the case of death at work.

(Xiaoyue, 18)

To improve the plight of the migrant workers, new laws must be enacted to help them. Labour contracts have been compulsory nationwide since 1995 for almost all forms of employment. Rising employment disputes have led to better regulations on labour dispute resolution since 1993 (China Statistical Yearbook, 2005). However, these two statutes are rarely applied or properly enforced in China. During the drafting stage of these two statutes, the Chinese government was perceived as adopting a pro-labour stance. That changed when a number of multinational companies and Chambers of Commerce threatened to pull out of China if these laws were seriously enforced.

Straight economics (therefore tax revenue) is perhaps the ultimate reason why local authorities tolerate highly polluting industries in their localities. Half the national tax base is in the state sector. In 2004, the private economy made up 60 per cent of the national economy and employed 75 per cent of the national workforce (China Statistical Yearbook, 2005). This explains why the migrant workers were the losers during the global supply chain and globalization era. Without government protection and with limited enforcement of labour laws, workers' marginalized social status has not been improved. The evolution of the global supply chain sets off more complicated job specifications. Wages remain low or below subsistence levels. The financial crisis is driving employers towards even more ruthless cost-cutting. Workers made jobless cannot or will not return to their hometowns because of similar dreadful working conditions. In their hometowns, the wages are even lower. Therefore, they prefer to remain in metropolitan areas. Yet, with meagre savings and no educational credentials or skills, migrant peasants are less employable than their more sophisticated urban peers. Of course, they want to earn enough money so that they can run a business or change their jobs to the service industry. But they lack the education needed to get a better job.

Taking into account the day-to-day conditions of factory life and the meagre pay given for such demanding work, the decision to partake in sex work is an embodiment of workers' agency under conditions where their options were severely limited. Moreover, in contrast to the conventional perception of rural woman being exploited, powerless victims of the global economy, the interviewees were fully conscious of their marginalization in post-reform China. They recognized the need to mobilize their resources to overcome their economic stagnancy. Making significantly more money is the deciding factor in pursuing sex work. While labour abuses and low pay are key motivators to leave factory life, many of the interviewees mentioned these factors as affecting their individualized self as well.

Making Sense of *Dagongmei*: From Retrenchment to Sex Work?

Clients routinely treat sex workers badly. The women endure verbal abuse as well as the risk of sexually transmitted diseases from clients who refuse to wear condoms. Xiaolin said that they tolerate these conditions because of the money:

> In the factory, I was exploited with such a disgraceful salary. Here in the nightclub, the pimps are exploiting me but it's not that bad and I can earn far higher wages.
>
> (Xiaolin, 23)

The streetwalkers are vulnerable to client-perpetrated violence, and some sex workers suffered different forms of sexual abuse from clients. Most of my interviewees work under different groups. Pimps guard them on the streets and introduce clients to them, then charge them commissions. They have to split the profits with the pimps, who usually take 60 per cent while the streetwalkers keep the other 40 per cent. Furthermore, streetwalkers are harassed by triad (gang) members who demand protection fees. Most of the streetwalkers did not want to work with a pimp, but it is the easiest way to increase business and, therefore, profit. Even if they did not work for the pimps, they would still have to deal with the triads. Also, if their pimps have a bad relationship with the police, the streetwalkers have to bribe both the police and the triad society because sex work is illegal in China.

Despite these conditions, most of them did not want to return to factory work. For example, Huiling said her pimp once raped her after she attempted to leave, but she still wants to stay in Dongguan as a streetwalker:

> I only wanted a happy and comfortable life when I made the decision to pursue sex work at that time.
>
> (Huiling, 20)

Masha, Xiangren, and Keyi also reported unpleasant experiences with their clients as streetwalkers, but all said they wanted to stay in the sex industry.

> I've been tied up and some clients would nip a cigarette bud on my breasts or my back …
>
> (Masha, 26)

> One client was so violent and dominant to control me. He poked holes in condom and had sex with me. I think it was all about the desire – the desire to be "bestialized." After that, I discovered that I was pregnant and I went for abortion … but I still want to stay in sex industry to enjoy the freedom and flexibility.
>
> (Xiangren, 21)

> Some clients have special requests like asking me to pee in front of them or strip dance. Some clients like objects so they like to kiss my underwear. The more excretion the panty has the happier they are. There are also some clients that like to smell my feet … some like S&M and foot jobs … Those are not easy jobs but I would rather stay in sex industry instead of going back to factory.
>
> (Keyi, 23)

Furthermore, those streetwalkers have to provide free sex to the police, since their pimps have to give "face" (status or credit) to the police in order to avoid arrest. Liaoyang said,

> Most policemen like rough sex, sometimes they'd show up around my neighbourhood and I'd give them free sexual services so they won't pester me. They like S&M or anything that's "extreme." One of them pushed a cigarette butt on my breasts and spine. But I want to survive so I did everything they asked for. That's the rule of China. This is China.
>
> (Liaoyang, 22)

Liaoyang told me that she had to bribe the police and triads for the sake of her own safety. Yanglin (28), from Chongqing, told me that before she went to work, she often went to a wet market to buy ducks, pigeons, or other small animals. She would kill the animals, collect their blood, and carry a piece of sponge soaked with blood to one of the designated low-end hotels where she served her clients. Just before sex, she would put the piece of sponge soaked with blood near her vagina. When the client noticed the blood afterwards, he would actually think Yanglin was still a virgin and give her extra money. Although Yanglin was constantly worried about catching diseases from this practice, the money made it difficult for her to stop.

Most of the sex workers complained about splitting the profits with the pimps. Over 80 per cent of my informants told me that they also had to provide free sex service to the pimps. They always experienced uninvited touching and kissing, where the clients pulled off their clothes and insulted their bodies. Over time, the accumulation of such bad experiences can deflate their self-esteem and result in job burnout.

Family Relationships of Sex Workers

From my conversations with the streetwalkers, all of them felt some shame and could not let their parents and family know that they were sex workers. Consequently, family members were alienated as they were seen to depersonalize and objectify their daughters as commodities. Sex work is "living off immoral earnings" in Chinese culture. For example, the husband of Wuchu (35) told her sister that she was a streetwalker, and her sister threatened to cut ties and disown her from the family. Still, Wuchu tried to keep contact with her family, since her parents helped her to take care of her son in her hometown. Over 40 out of 45 streetwalkers capitalized on money as a tool, which mingled with Confucian values so that they could fulfil their roles both as filial, pious daughters and mothers, and as individualized selves. These conversations also exposed the dilemmas facing breadwinning peasant sex workers who must hide how they earned their income. They regularly experienced moral qualms, guilt, and shame. But these negative feelings were offset by the autonomy, freedom, and individualized self attained through the tangible reward of adequate remuneration.

The Allure of Sex Work in the Global City: Cosmopolitan Individuals

Remaining in the commercial sex industry is not a perfect choice, but the significantly higher income allows workers to refashion and reorient their identities. This is valuable, since the "personal" reflects a post-reform state discourse on developing the neoliberal "personal" identity, which stands in stark contrast to Mao-era conceptualizations of the "collective." The significance of the "personal" is not only perpetuated by way of a culture of neoliberalism but also propagated by the state discourse of the individualized self. Arguably, the migration process and eventual participation in sex work are the first instances where migrant women are offered the opportunity to explore a distinct identity outside of their family. Sex work gives them recreational time, disposable income, and the particular freedoms that come when leaving home. In effect, both migration and their newly acquired economic freedoms allow these women to experience and recognize themselves as a "modern subject." The transition from rural farm girl to city factory worker then to financially secure sex worker is important in understanding how these women see themselves within the context of a hyper-competitive labour market. In line with Parreñas's (2011a, 2011b) findings, these women recognize that their transition to relative financial security and upward economic mobility is made possible through sex work. Therefore, while sex work poses some distinct hardships, it nevertheless offers these migrant women the possibility of achieving upward mobility and "personal growth" that would not otherwise be possible.

Migrant sex workers devote a percentage of their earnings to fashionable lifestyles even as they seek to secure their economic futures. When asked what she enjoyed doing with her earnings, Meixia says,

> My friend from Hong Kong invited me to dinner. I was so excited. We went to a Western restaurant and I was completely ignorant of restaurants, let alone the etiquette. I didn't know how to use a knife and fork. Even worse, I don't know how to order because the dishes shown on the menu were new to me. After this experience, I learned how to surf the internet whenever I'm free. That was how I learned to eat with a knife and fork. I'm now more civilized and modern. It's hard to believe that life here in the city can be so much more meaningful even if it means that I have to work as a prostitute to enjoy eating in a restaurant.
>
> (Meixia, 22)

Most of the streetwalkers said they are happy to have choice and control of their life. Meihua highlights how her salary allows her to reframe and understand her "self" in a manner that would not have been possible if she had continued working at the factory:

> I try to look more modern and cosmopolitan; then, my customers believe that I'm worth what they paid for. I can buy cosmetic products, stylish clothes, and attractive accessories to make me look more modern and cosmopolitan ... With money, I can hire a dermatologist to cure my skin allergy and I look more confident ...
>
> (Meihua, 22)

I stay in the sex industry because I can enjoy freedom and autonomy. I only work 22 days per month, but I can earn more than 9,000 yuan [US$1,304] per month ... I can take leave whenever I want. Unlike working in a factory 7 days per week, 30 days per month, where I was paid less than 2,000 yuan [US$435] ...

(Shenman, 34)

Xinmei also says,

I bought an apartment in Dongguan in 2008 ... The property market is good and I enjoy the profits a lot. I like my job as I can spend ... Sex work brings me happiness, dignity, status, and friendship. I have developed friendship with other sisters [streetwalkers]. When clients refuse to pay and become rude, my sister will call the pimps and we can help each other out ... If I feel lonely and sad, my sisters comfort me ... My life has meaning again ...

(Xinmei, 24)

Xiaofang also says,

I was lucky. I bought an apartment in Wuhan in 2009. It cost me only 300,000 yuan (US$50,000) and I rent it out to support my parents' expenses in Wuhan ... It is a high-rise building, not a mud or brick house. My parents have never seen a skyscraper before. I enjoy saving and investing in property. I have a dream, I want to become a businesswoman. And I still have hope to find a good husband ...

(Xiaofang, 30)

Money is the king. So, if I have money, people won't have contempt for me. Whoever has money is one who will receive respect and prestige in society. I can take control of my own life ...

(Dingding, 24)

Because of the various negative connotations behind money earned from working in the commercial sex industry, most participants conceal the source of their income from family and friends. But they nevertheless flaunt their savings as a mechanism of ego defence and individualization. In the rural areas where most of the low-end sex workers come from, money is the ultimate measure of success: "Everyone knows what it means to be rich." When returning to their rural villages, participants use their money openly and symbolically to purchase property and/or gold jewellery. In this way they earn face and respect for their family and themselves in the village. Material items that are purchased with money are imbued with symbolic value, and money becomes a way for villagers and family members to quantify, acknowledge, and evaluate a worker's success.

Another way to establish one's modernity and individualized self is learning how to eat Western food. Knowing how to eat with a knife and fork and even surfing the internet are products of modernity that are forging the streetwalker's reflexive individuality. The pursuit of fashion and style is illustrative of how a peasant woman's acquisition of money through sex work provides her with the means to reconstruct herself "as a reflexive and inward-directed source of valuation" (Sassatelli, 2000, pp. 215–16), untrammelled by collective bonds in the countryside that can no longer provide for her financial well-being. It is not unreasonable to suggest that the peasant sex workers' intention to treat their money as an intermediary of potential (Deflem, 2003) allows them to widen their spheres of choice and underwrite their financial futures. At a grander scale, the financial success of the sex workers fuels the fragmentation and ongoing de-collectivization of rural China.

In effect, money and economic mobility offer the opportunity to become a "better" self. For most of the streetwalkers, money allows them to make consumer choices which position them as "modern." Rather than simple farm girls, these women can present themselves as successful cosmopolites, able to purchase items such as magazines, skin-care products, and fashionable clothing. Sex work allows migrant women to be situated in the middle or "centre" of the dominant urban social milieu in a manner previously unattainable (Hsu, 2005, p. 553).

Many of the women also explained how moving to the city allowed them to end situations of domestic abuse by their husbands. Some women described their home lives as an oppressive dictatorship. They felt they had to endure physical and verbal abuse because of their financial dependence upon their male partners. In moving away from the village and into the city, most of these women left their children with their parents to ensure a safe and stable environment. This enabled these women to renegotiate their social positions as they improved their financial situations. Even before these women came to Dongguan, the demands of family life and heteronormative expectations were critical structures impacting their decision-making processes. Segueing to sex work in Guangdong province has therefore proven to be the most financially viable option for these women who determined they had to resist returning to their rural milieu.

Conclusion

This chapter contextualized how *dagongmei*-turned-sex-workers negotiate their lives within the constraints of contemporary China. Without the support of recognized institutional bodies (the formal labour market, government-instituted services), and with the expectations placed upon them through social dictates (individualized self, freedom, and autonomy), the significance of income earned through sex work cannot be overstated. In effect, similar to Parreñas's model (2011a), these women may not be beholden to the dictates of exploitative contracts but rather are *bounded* to societal expectations and limited forms of social and material support. This situation places women within a framework wherein sex work is one of the few platforms that enables them to overcome their socio-economic environment and attain upward economic mobility. In this context, engaging in sex work is a rational and acceptable response.

These material and social structures and situational contexts frame the sex workers' choices as "bounded," insofar as their choices are not made in a vacuum or where possibilities are plentiful. Simply because choice is limited and fraught with a complex socio-economic context, one cannot discount that these choices are deliberate. By understanding the material conditions of migrant labour and how the social forces of individualized self become underlying motivators that lead women into sex work, this chapter unearths the complex subjective discourses and political and economic realities that frame how these decisions are made.

Officially sanctioned labour unions and political elites of China remain unwilling to fight for the rights of these poor streetwalkers and low-end sex workers. Labour law protection remains inadequate. The Chinese government gives some concessions to multinational corporations but is less concerned about the well-being of migrant workers. Therefore, the limited enforcement of these and other pieces of legislation has exacerbated the marginalization of these migrant sex workers. The women with whom I spoke candidly admitted that they could do little about these irrefragable circumstances regarding class and economic identities. But they remain determined to continue in sex work until they have amassed sufficient funds to retire and return to their village to start a business or pursue other options through individualization. There is nevertheless a challenge that needs to be addressed. Most of the *dagongmei* whom I interviewed saw prostitution as a nonpermanent work arrangement and vowed to withdraw when they have saved enough money.

Furthermore, regardless of whether these women participate in the formal or informal sector, without urban *hukou* these women receive limited support and recognition from local governments. They are denied access to public services, basic welfare, health care, and affordable public housing. These women recognize that there is little support for them from institutions such as the formal labour market and the government. But by and large, the streetwalkers I interviewed were satisfied with being bounded by their material, social, and cultural demands to achieve their goals. Despite being embedded in a labour market that failed to provide them with adequate employment or opportunity, they found a way to hope. Through sex work they saw themselves as upwardly mobile, independent, and free.

Chapter 3 looks at the single-adult migrant men and at entangled masculinity in China's commercial sex industry. The focus is on the relationship between sex workers and clients in low-end and mid-tier niche markets. These men face a crisis in terms of their masculine identity in today's China, and buying commercial sex is a way they try to cope.

Chapter Three

Disappointed and Despondent: How Young-Adult Male Migrants Contest Masculinity in China's Low-End and Mid-Tier Niche Markets

Jiang is a factory worker whom I met in the Peach Bar several times. He loved staying at this bar because he feels lost in his job. One night in summer 2016, he looked very desperate and tired, and I said, "Can I buy you a drink?" He nodded his head and found it amazing that someone had offered to buy him a drink. After he had his drink, he started talking to me. He said,

> I am working in a garment industry like a slave! I am competing for a job with women. They are teasing and giggling in front of me and said I am a garbage! My mother called me twice per day to urge me to get married in my hometown. She said all my peers in my hometown had already married and have already two kids! I did not have time to date a girl as I work over 12 hours per day. I even cannot afford to have a girlfriend as I only receive 4,000 yuan [US$645] per month. The gender imbalance make man redundant in China. Most of the factory girls in my factory are looking for some local rich guy or middle-class managers. They are not interested in me. The stress makes me feel I have to run away from my family, my factory, and staying in this bar and make myself drunk. I won't save anymore. At any rate, I won't say much and why I have to force myself to have a frugal life? Why I don't pamper myself and spending all savings on buying commercial sex? I love the feeling to be pampered, indulged, and manly when I am around the sex workers.
>
> (Jiang, 28)

Jiang told me that he is a controlling and dominant person. He has strong sexual desires. Each month he spends one-third of his monthly salary on cheap sex. He uses women's bodies to affirm his masculinity. He likes to grab the sex worker's head and – despite her struggles – force her to take his seed into her mouth. He expects women to perform overtly feminine roles like appearing half-nude or fully nude with candles. This erotic environment enhances his sense of masculinity. Jiang articulates a sense of superiority by buying the sex services of women. He enjoys the sex workers who demurely pour beer, caress his arm or shoulder, and flirt with him. The sex workers in the Peach Bar help him achieve a sense of being "attractive" and "almighty" in the public sphere. And sex workers' jobs include admiring his body, giving him "face," and boosting his confidence. The sex service provided by the women in the Peach Bar disguises his economic anxiety and insecurity as a factory worker in China.

This chapter focuses on clients who buy commercial sex in the low-end markets of the Peach Bar and Lotus Club. Single-adult male migrants are rarely treated as a distinct analytical category in research interventions in the burgeoning area of migration and sexuality. As China's global influence continues to rise, so also interest in its sociocultural trends rises as well. The study of the intersectionality of masculinity, migration, and sexuality in China and East Asia remains in a nascent state. The male purchase of commercial sex is often neglected in studies of internal migration, labour, and masculinity: such men have hidden themselves from researchers because of the stigma and illegality attached to the payment for sex. Consequently, there is a dearth of scholarship on how single-adult migrant clients negotiate their masculinities when buying commercial sex, or on the link between urban migration and buying commercial sex. This chapter extends Connell's hegemonic masculinity and addresses an under-researched aspect of subaltern masculinities. The resultant masculinity crisis within this group expresses itself in three major "entangled" life tensions from which the Chinese single-adult male migrants find it difficult to escape: first, there is tension between their low wages and a patriarchal family norm that expects a higher income before a man is socially approved to marry and have children; second, there is the tension of the dominant discourse in urban China, which marks male migrants as failures in a society that equates success and status with having wealth; and third, there is a tension arising from the culturally marginalizing behaviour of soliciting prostitutes for sexual pleasure and physical release. The crisis associated by this simultaneity of different social positions and accompanying masculinities and femininities is driven by China's economic reforms and *hukou* (household registration) reforms. The *hukou* reform enables and promotes mass internal migration from inland China to coastal cities. A historical factor is the one-child policy, which has generated a substantial gender imbalance in the young Chinese population.

Domestic migrants have been branded as "the floating population" (*liudong renkou* 流動人口) in China. Government figures estimate that there are between 100 and 150 million of these single-adult males subsisting at the bottom of the workforce (National Bureau of Statistics of China, 2016). In 2007, in Guangdong province alone, the shortage of female labour was 1,398,579 individuals. Meanwhile, the percentage of male employees increased from 42 per cent in 2004 to 53.9 per cent in 2012 (National Bureau of Statistics of China, 2013). In addition, in 2014 the gender ratio at birth was 115.88 boys to every 100 girls (Huang, 2015). In 2014, of the approximately 170,000 people aged 20–59 who were single in China, men outnumbered women by 104,000 (59.6 per cent) to 70,000 (40.4 per cent). According to the report, the percentages for single men aged 20–34, 35–39, and 40–45 were 67.3 per cent, 69.4 per cent, and 66.3 per cent, respectively. To meet the sexual impulses of so many single unattached men, a thriving and robust sex industry has emerged across social strata. This chapter focuses on clients who buy commercial sex in the low-end market (the Peach Bar) and mid-tier bar (the Lotus Club).

Conceptualizing Masculinity

Traditional views of men as hunter-gatherers, aggressive decision-makers, and dominant and successful have been reassessed as research indicates that many stereotypes are false and inaccurate. Studies of global masculinities focus on the agency of subaltern groups (Spivak, 1995). The global markets are gendered because Western elite males are in charge of directing capital flows through leading institutions like the International Monetary Fund (IMF) or the World Bank, but the study of global masculinities focuses on tension produced through economic change and the formation of marginalized masculinities (Connell, 1995). The men left behind are forced to assume so-called feminized roles, such as domestic workers, clerks, and service personnel. Migrant workers in particular must struggle with new configurations of masculinity as a result of the institutionalization of women's rights (Wyrod, 2008). In studying this activity in southern China, I present the masculinities of China's rural subaltern population in terms of the different social positions people simultaneously occupy and navigate. It is important for scholars to consider the ways in which these social categories inflect by talking about power relationally. Consequently, the study of masculinity in this chapter is focused on single male migrants and addresses the following questions. 1) Among migrant men, what constitutes masculinity and why is it important? 2) How has China's post-socialist transition fuelled a so-called masculinity crisis among migrant men? 3) In what way does using commercial sex help migrants assert their masculinity? 4) In what ways does it help the migrants find their lost masculinity?

The masculinities of "surplus populations" are under-theorized (Cowen & Siciliano, 2011). This book is a new perspective on understanding how simultaneous masculinities and desires are differentially articulated and shaped by external economic, institutional, and demographic changes, as well as by heteronormative expectations in China. Connell's work on hegemonic masculinity is fascinating; however, she ignores different phantasms of masculinities and the links between macro-arguments of political economy. In other words, how does the way that the individual constructs masculinity directly link it to the economy and political development? A masculinity crisis is emerging in China's modernizing urban societies. It is being driven by China's economic and *hukou* (household registration) reforms that, according to Connell's (2016, p. 312) argument, make it impossible to impose any single gender template when it comes to understanding the changed hegemonic project of masculinity formation within the global South. In light of Connell's reference to how the metropole-apparatus of colonial power structures contests masculinities in allowing for overseas trade and the continued exploitation of Third World nations, a parallel can be drawn with how China's urban reform promotes mass internal migration from inland China to the coastal cities. This, along with the gender imbalance discussed earlier, results in the production of a "surplus population" and its concomitant masculinities.

Taking a cue from the concepts of subaltern masculinities (Connell, 1995; Spivak, 1995) and devalorized masculinity (Cowen & Siciliano, 2011), I argue that the masculinity crisis of the single and young migrants is entwined with the trajectories of economic change in post-reform China. The masculinity crisis of those migrants includes a variety of masculine phantasms which co-exist, resulting in a complex interplay of masculinities which are tied to the post-socialist transition that has reshaped China's social structure, economy, and culture. In Connell's recent work, she argues that the relationship between hegemony and masculinities is increasingly contested because of changing structures of power in light of the decolonization of the global South (Connell, 2016). Cutting-edge research interventions by Mac an Ghaill and Haywood (2007) have transcended the empirical contextualization of hegemonic masculinities and moved towards theorizing the relationality of masculinity with other social categories. Mac an Ghaill and Haywood (2007) implied that power, difference, and desire are mapped out not only in terms of gender but also in terms of other social and cultural identifications, such as ethnicity, sexuality, and class.

In China, parallels can be drawn with the single-adult male migrants who are undoubtedly negotiating the crisis of devalorization by taking up forms of employment, usually associated with female labour, that are subsequently exploited. Thus, my work captures how the migrant men address this devalorization by procuring sex.

In the case of China, the growth of an urban middle class has resulted in the masculinities of rural men being subjected to contest. Rather than being the beneficiaries of economic reform and globalization, rural men are actually the losers, lacking the wherewithal to get married and form a family. Family reproduction is a socio-political issue in China and single-adult migrants have few opportunities to improve their status. Faced with limited options for finding partners or girlfriends, they find commercial sex to be the most viable choice. The revalorization of single male migrants takes on a particular classed and gendered transformation in China's neoliberal trajectories. The life tension in the trajectories of economic reform and globalization make these men redundant (McDowell, 2003), surplus population, and they suffer from devalorized masculinity. This form of valorized masculinity is not just related to men who have to work but also reflects a classed and gendered process in that they are being marginalized. This chapter identifies five categories of behaviour whereby men rationalize and assert their masculinity: vigorous and macho; suppressive and anxious; fantasy and bounded; extravagant and competitive; and bragging and collaborative. These phantasms are interactional and represent personas adopted by men when relating to women within a specific context.

Post-Socialist Transition in China

The cultural significance of sex work in post-socialist China is but one of the many consequences of events leading up to and including the global financial crisis of 2008. Most of the women could work near their hometowns, since most of the factories had been moving to the interior part of China because of cheap land rent and an abundant supply of land. Women prefer to work closer to their hometowns, where they can take care of their children and enjoy more emotional attachment with their families. This provides an opportunity for unskilled and low-educated young men to fill in the employment void, even though they are unwilling to accept feminized jobs.

Getting rich remains the dominant value for men in China, and many are seeking to manipulate women's bodies to contest their masculinity. Within the context of the growing consumer revolution that has followed the global financial crisis, China's hyper-materialism has melded with the importance of hegemonic masculinity under the patriarchal system. According to Kavanaugh (2015), the masculinity crisis is related to structural changes and cultural context. Against the backdrop of burgeoning economic growth throughout the past several years, the concept that men should become the sole breadwinners has established itself as a core tenet of broader public value within Chinese society.

The single-adult migrants generate different phantasms of masculinities that intersect with their major "entangled" life tensions. Buying commercial sex enables them to find their lost masculinity and articulate a voice. The different phantasms of masculinities are tied to the post-socialist transition which has reshaped China's social structure, economy, and culture.

In China, forming a family and reproducing has been a socio-political issue. In the Maoist era, young and poor men with inferior class backgrounds were regarded as threats to the socialist revolution. The Chinese Communist Party used certain biopolitical techniques to maintain the purity of the "revolutionary army" and created obstacles that prevented poor men from marginalized classes from finding spouses or satisfying their sexual desires, in order to prevent them from "polluting" the revolutionaries via reproduction (Zhang, 2015, p. 819).

Different Masculinity Phantasms

In post-socialist China, single-adult migrants are in a desperate battle to get rid of their underprivileged class labels because there are few opportunities for them to climb up to the upper hierarchy and improve their intergenerational mobility. Consequently, they may turn to commercial sex services as a quick release that is more attainable than finding girlfriends. In this context, the behaviours and attitudes expressed by these men conform to stereotypical male phantasms because they are accessible, easy to adopt, and the script is familiar to the women being solicited. There are five specific patterns of behaviour whereby male clients rationalize and assert their masculinity:

1 Vigorous and macho (repressive and lascivious behaviour such as groping, tickling, sadism, and indifferent deceit), which is limited to sexually oriented activities;
2 Fantasy and bounded (different forms of intimate physical contact

such as kissing and caressing, which blur the boundaries between commercial sex and non-commercial sex), with fantasy-oriented activities;

3 Anxious and suppressive (reluctant displays of normative, heterosexual manliness to suppress queer desire), with suppressive-oriented activities;

4 Extravagant and competitive (displays of conspicuous consumption such as buying alcohol and expensive food to make a point, and buying flowers, jewellery, and other goods to demonstrate financial power or authority);

5 Bragging and collaborative (showing off physical attractiveness; getting VIP rooms at bars; excessive alcohol intake; and the ability to collaborate with the bosses and pimps to assert masculinity).

The five phantasms I suggest are not firmly defined static constructs. They are more like personas adopted by men when relating to women within a specific context. Monthly income is a crucial social metric in China for determining whether a man can even afford to get married. According to the National Bureau of Statistics of China (2015), in Shenzhen, a man must have a salary of at least 15,920 yuan (US$2,341) per month; in Guangzhou it is 8,785 yuan (US$1,291); in Beijing it is 14,900 yuan (US$2,191); and in Shanghai it is 12,065 yuan (US$1,774). But for migrants, the mean monthly salary in 2015 was only 2,864 yuan (US$461), less than half of the 2016 median income (5,868 yuan, US$862) of city *hukou* residents in Dongguan (one of China's top 10 cities in 2014). Therefore, marriage-minded women generally won't consider workers as possible partners. Migrant men know that their prospects are bleak, and they have few options for relationships or intimacy outside of inexpensive sex workers and streetwalkers. This study fills a gap in our understanding of masculinities and in turn links it to the backdrop of China's post-socialist transition, economic reform, and globalization.

The Masculinity Crisis: Pressure from Parents to Get Married

Beyond the distinct culture of the factory, the priority placed on finding a proper spouse continues to be a significant social issue in China. The preference for male offspring, coupled with years of a one-child family planning policy, resulted in skewed birth ratios. The situation is even worse for those with low-salary factory jobs. Within urban China, it is not unusual to see anxious parents from rural communities assuming the role of matchmakers trying to find a suitable wife for their son. These parents generally cannot afford the minimum fee of 8,000 yuan (US$1,194) that matrimonial agencies typically charge. So they gather at matchmaking corners in public parks and amusement centres in cities throughout Guangdong province; they share photos and contact information of their unwed male adult children, who are colloquially referred to as "leftovers." Anxious faces and exaggerated body language reveal the enthusiasm and agitation of parents, adamant to find a spouse for their sons. Staying single into and beyond one's late-20s is still considered improper. Moreover, the expectation of getting married and having a family is not merely a concern between parents and their adult children; marriage remains a significant societal norm. Parents act as matchmakers at marriage markets and large-scale speed-dating events that are now regularly scheduled in almost every Chinese city.

My respondents faced added challenges because their older ages, precarious work, and low salaries made them less desirable partners. Furthermore, these men faced an added layer of emasculation because they occupied "feminine jobs."

How Do Male Migrants Contest Masculinity in China's Commercial Sex Industry?

Fang, a male migrant worker from Anhui, discussed the pressures surrounding marriage:

> My mom spends all her time organizing blind dates for me. She repeatedly tells me that a son who won't get married in rural China is a sin and shame! Our whole family and kin will be punished. It might be that our family has done something wrong ...
>
> (Fang, 34)

Workplace tensions faced by male migrants are exacerbated by the pressures of failing to meet family responsibilities regarding marriage and childbearing, which remain dictated and enforced by parental authority (Choi & Luo, 2016). This pressure is compounded by the expectation that the sole gateway to childbearing is marriage. According to a 2006 nationwide general social survey, about 50 per cent of Chinese claimed that married people should bear children; around 45 per cent agreed that it is necessary to have a son to carry on the family name; and 68.5 per cent agreed that family happiness was more important than individual interests (Choi & Luo, 2016). The notion of a loveless and primarily pragmatic marriage is not viewed as problematic within a

Chinese context; intergenerational harmony, rather than conjugal love, is deemed essential for the family (Watson & Ebrey, 1991). Additionally, within rural China, marriage is often framed as a functional step towards maintaining family inheritance (Choi & Luo, 2016).

For many of the men I interviewed, finding a girlfriend and getting married were top priorities. These men are expected to purchase a house, get married, and continue their family bloodline; these markers of adulthood are part of the narrative of being a good son and, therefore, a good man. Sun, an only child from Hunan, shares his stress:

> I still think that failing to get married is a sign of a bad son and disrespectful to my parents. Who is going to inherit my bloodline [*xiemai*]? I lose *lian* [face] in front of my relatives and family members in Spring Festival. My neighbours even think my ancestors did something wrong and so my family doesn't have offspring to prolong our bloodline. My mom asks me to get a good girl from the countryside and marry soon. The criteria for a good girl by her definition are fertile, docile, have baby fat, and be young ...
>
> (Sun, 34)

Failure to attain these markers of normative adult manhood do not merely reflect negatively on the family unit but also speak to a perceived failure of one's heteronormative male identity. The inability to adequately participate in these heteronormative cultural rituals shapes the overall identity of these men. This pressure reaches its zenith during New Year celebrations when migrants return home and relatives relentlessly pry into their personal lives. Xiaodong, a migrant from Sichuan, recalls his experience:

> Last year, when I go home during Chinese New Year, I rented a girl from our factory and asked her to act like my girlfriend. I rented her service for seven days and paid her 200 yuan [US$30] per day. My parents were very delighted to see my girlfriend and urged me to get married soon. My mother keeps reminding me a man who is over 39 and comes from rural China – but is still single – is a curse to my kin and ancestors ...
>
> (Xiaodong, 39)

Strained relationships due to financial pressures were common among the interviewees. Factory worker Xu, 36, recalled the first meeting with his girlfriend's parents in Chongqing during the winter of 2014. His girlfriend's parents asked about his salary and potential marriage plans. When Xu informed his future mother-in-law that it was not practical for him to buy a house at that time, she advised her daughter to end the relationship. Ye (32), a garment factory worker, noted a common truism: "Women cannot feed a family with just love." He said that men are expected to provide women with material comforts and practical needs, especially a house. Jie shared points of stress from his previous relationships:

> My ex-girlfriends commonly ask questions like do you have a house or are you living with parents? What is your job? How much did you earn? Do you have a car? Are you a professional? It is very difficult to find girls who want to eat in KFC or McDonald's. I have three "lows," low salary, low status, and low height ...
>
> (Jie, 35)

There were several interviewees who felt that normative monogamous relationships were hardly ideal. Liming, a factory working in his mid-30s, said that his demanding work schedule made it difficult to pursue or maintain a conventional relationship. As a result, he avoided long-term romantic obligations and conventional emotional attachments.

Buying Commercial Sex as Phantasy

Single-adult male migrants negotiate distinct anxieties such as pressure from parents to get married and start a family as well as coping with feelings of emasculation from their work. Most if not all the interviewees agreed that they purchased sex in order to ease the sense of unhappiness from their devalorized jobs and pressure from their families to perform the masculinities required. The various and often contradictory reasons for buying sex cannot be easily organized using a single index but can be tied down to a phantasmology. The notion of phantasy is imagined as a scene of disidentification (Mac an Ghaill & Haywood, 2007, p. 145). For these factory boys facing a masculinity crisis, purchasing sex from prostitutes helps them disidentify with their emasculated professions. In the words of Butler (1993, p. 22), "Identities operate ... through the discursive construction of a constitutive outside ... of abjected and marginalized subjects ... which return to trouble and unsettle the foreclosures which we prematurely call 'identities.'" She therefore states that the foreclosures that constitute identities "are phantasmatic efforts at alignment" (ibid). Taking a cue from my data and the literature, the five phantasms that are deployed to help the factory boys disidentify with their feminized occupations emerged from this group of interviewees. These are not mutually exclusive, and each interviewee may manifest more than one in any given instance.

Vigorous and Macho Phantasms

Behaviours associated with violence, aggression, coercion, machismo, and active suppression of emotion or empathetic care for sex workers were most common. Most of the male migrants called themselves "chicken worms" (*jichong* 雞蟲), which literally means men who frequently patronize female sex workers. There was a recurrent tendency to discuss predilections towards rough sex and sadomasochism to contest hegemonic masculinity. By purchasing sex, these men experienced gratification through acts they would otherwise probably not experience. As Xiaodong, a 39-year-old construction worker, succinctly highlighted, "It's all about control and conquering." Xiaodong regularly purchased sex services specializing in S&M (sadomasochism), rough sex, or anything considered "extreme." This included tying up the worker and flipping lit cigarette butts onto her breasts and back. Many of the men in my study noted that sex with sex workers was distinctly more aggressive and self-serving than the sexual interactions they had with romantic partners. Luo also highlighted the difference between sex with a dating partner and that with a sex worker:

> I only want wild sex with the sex workers. I have the wildest libido and dreams that excite me. My friend called me "jueqingdao" [絕情刀, literally cruel and hungry for sex] because I have a very strong sex appetite. I use those sex workers for pleasure and happiness ... I am a typical "hit and run" person ... I don't want to have trouble ...
>
> (Luo, 34)

These migrants stressed that purchasing sex allowed them to make their personal wants and desires a priority. For many of these men, the emphasis on their personal gratification was directly linked to domination, aggression, and control. Conversely, they stressed the importance of their female partner being submissive and demure. Most of these men explored power dynamics and accessed vigorous and hyper-masculine identities through sex. Additionally, many of these men were reluctant to discuss sex as an emotional and personal experience. Instead, sex was framed in terms of drive and as a fulfilling yet intrinsic biological necessity. The respondents were also quick to note the importance of the woman's physical appearance.

Lihao (34) spends 1,800 of his total 4,000 yuan (US$588) on commercial sex each month. He beamed with pride and satisfaction about his experiences. He bragged that he had hired as many as six girls over the course of one night. Besides his sexual prowess, he also highlighted the importance of the social elements of these relationships. He stated that sex workers took the initiative to develop their connections with him. They listened to his stories attentively, laughed at his jokes, and praised him. Although these gestures may not be authentic, the interactions make Lihao feel respected, admired, and masculine. In the bar, he likes to publicly fondle the sex worker by pulling her blouse up to expose her breast. When she covers up in (feigned) embarrassment, it makes him laugh. Another game Lihao plays in public is putting a cherry or grape on the girl's breast and using it as an excuse to eat it, and then sucking her nipple. Still another game is to put his mobile phone in vibrate mode and place it on the girl's breasts to make her squeal. These games enable Lihao to construct a masculinity which distracts him from his feelings of marginalization and emasculation in other areas of his life. The sex workers in low-end and mid-tier bars pretend to be docile and capitalize on their beauty and body to get more money. Sex workers play a crucial role in helping the single-adult male migrants reinvent themselves in China. It is a calculated strategy between workers and clients, and the girls treat this relationship as theatre following a script. Sex workers lie to the migrants and tell them that they are superior. Women creatively use their bodies and flirtation skills to keep clients returning.

Fantasy and Bounded Phantasms

Fantasy and bounded phantasms refer to fantasy-oriented activities between clients and sex workers that psychically create an imagined scene of stability where masculine dominance is the norm. For these men, buying commercial sex does not solely fulfil their libidinal needs and psychological loneliness; rather, these exchanges are premised on satisfying the more abstract components of clients' emotions (Kong, 2015a, p. 816). These clients foster "bounded intimacy," a form of intimacy that is real yet rarely crosses the boundaries of contractual exchange. Milrod and Weitzer (2012, p. 454) describe this type of client-worker relationship as a "paid relationship" or "a genuine but limited sexual and emotional experience." Men who embody bounded masculinity know and enjoy the rules of this clear commercial transaction.

Ruanji says that the sex workers he has met are docile, sexually open, and expressive (*wenyou* 溫柔). He finds those girls sexually arousing and says that they know how to soothe his ego and relax him. Ruanji openly admits that he knows the girls lie to him just to feed his ego. They adopt overtly submissive feminine roles and tell him he is hot, sexy, and manly. These interactions enable Ruanji to reconstruct a self-image of powerful manliness which helps him cope with the lack of power over his stagnant economic and social situation. Ruanji says,

> I know I shall not fall in love with Shanshan [low-end sex worker, aged 23]. I could only donate my sperm but not my love [*liujing bu liuqing* 留精不留情]. I confess "sunken boat" [*dachenchuan* 搭沉船, literally "there is no true love in prostitution"] is risky and dangerous. My friend told me I am an old fool and I am sinking. She is very caring and submissive. I love licking, hugging, touching, talking, and fucking with her ... I know I have to be detached and run away ... one day I know I will do that ...
>
> (Ruanji, 39)

Jianjun is a factory worker. He likes those girls he has met. He says he could easily be involved with an eighteen-year-old young and "spicy" girl (*zhengmei* 正妹). He says,

> I like Huifang [low-end sex worker, aged 18] and we have certain chemistry and we connect well. In gazing into her eyes, I can lose myself ... She offers me lots of off-the-clock activities and special favours to me like texting me for birthday ... it makes me feel I am a king [*daye* 大爺] special and I can't help taking this challenge ...
>
> (Jianjun, 39)

> ... She changed a lot after being with me including her wardrobe choices and her resting time. I was broke and she bought me beer, cigarettes, meal, and paid for my living expenses for three months ... She is pregnant and I will become a dad soon. She is trying to be a good wife, but I still haven't overcome my hurdle to marry a sex worker as a wife ... She did not charge me when we have sex later ... I only want the baby to fulfil my parents' expectation ...
>
> (Ruokang, 37)

This fantasy indirectly encourages Ruokang and others to spend one-third of their monthly salary at the low-end bar with the hope of maintaining their fantasy "celebrity" status. Under the romantic aura of a so-called private relationship, the quality and performance of a sex worker not only indicate a man's economic power but also convey class privilege, although most of the migrants admitted that they were mediocre and not attractive. However, they are happy to spend their precious monthly income on premium commercial sex services (*diye fuwu* 大爺服務) and their class-code masculinity. Zhenyong is a 34-year-old factory worker and he comes from a small village in Qingdao. He likes sex workers in the bar who flirt with him by touching his arm, pouring him drinks, and gazing attentively at him. A substantial number (over 70 per cent) of the male migrant workers interviewed wanted to have children with the sex workers. However, most of these men will not marry low-end sex workers because of loss of "face." Zhenyong said that those girls help him project an image of masculine potency and sexual attractiveness when he comes to the bar. Their appearance helps their clients achieve a sense of being "attractive" and "almighty" through their interactions.

Anxious and Suppressive Phantasms

Other behaviours of male migrants are associated with active emotional suppression, anxiety, or lack of empathetic care. Jiang (23) admitted that he pays for a range of sexual activities at the Peach Bar depending upon his feeling that day – including flirtation, erotic performance ("heavy petting"), hand jobs, fellatio, and sexual intercourse. He agreed that these help mask his loneliness and admits that he is anxious about the precarious factory job he has in Dongguan. During our conversation he admitted that he likes the "cheap look" of sex workers. He admitted that this is about his suppression and the fear of being marginalized in the marriage market. He uses a biological essentialism to articulate that access to sex is a "fundamental human right," mobilizing the aesthetic of universalism. Jiang was cognizant that sex workers often construct professional identities that match male fantasies of a submissive woman willing to cater to male desires. Arguably, it is within these exchanges that customers can purchase an experience to act out a highly normative gender dynamic. In effect, these exchanges enable men who experience emasculation in other parts of their life to perform a vigorous and hyper-macho identity.

Luoyang, a bisexual factory worker who has stayed in Dongguan for four years, discussed his desire to "dominate" female sex workers as a means of releasing his anxiety about working in a factory. He says,

> I had a plastic whip, candles and plastic cuffs. I also wear some studded long boots ... I love being a dominant "top." I play music from my phone, and invite the girl to dance in front of me, give me a strip tease and dance ... It makes me wild and fly [*xingfen* 興奮].
>
> (Luoyang, 36)

I would nip a cigarette bud on the girl's breast. I also like to bring as many girls as I like 10-P [nine sex workers and him]. There are lots of combinations, sometimes it could be four clients and six bar girls ... I forget the reality of my pain and anxiety ...

(Ji, 37)

EXTRAVAGANT AND COMPETITIVE PHANTASMS

Wangkai is a factory worker from Wuhan. Although he only earns 7,000 yuan (US$1,129) per month as a technician in Dongguan, he estimates that he spends around one-third of his monthly salary to pay for commercial sex services. Wangkai enjoys VIP client status in the Lotus Club. He says,

I pay so much money to buy the VIP membership from Lotus Club. If I pay 600 yuan [US$97], Kevin will arrange a VIP room for me to avoid the attention from the police. I feel very superior when compared to the other men who cannot afford this service.

(Wangkai, 32)

Other displays of extravagance include buying brand-name handbags for the girls. Wangkai shows off by spending additional money to have a girl sit with him. The minimum charge to get the table next to the prettiest girl (young, curvy, and with cultural capital) was US$91 in the Lotus Club with a VIP room. Visiting sex workers in groups is a common form of homosocial bonding and fraternity between these single-adult migrants. It was observed that the migrants mostly discussed how their participation in these spaces was tied to maintaining a class-based masculinity in front of their peers. Their sense of pride is also elevated when paying the bill for the evening and seeing who received the most attention from the best bar girls in the Lotus Club.

Jiahuan is a 28-year-old truck driver in Dongguan. He described how to use alcohol or champagne to show off in front of his peer groups when buying commercial sex in a mid-tier or low-end bar. He ordered bottles of extravagant and imported champagne. The girl would give a client a kiss and a hug if he could afford to pay the most expensive bill for the night. These men make a show of success by spending large sums to consume Western luxury goods even though they can scarcely afford it.

BRAGGING AND COLLABORATIVE PHANTASMS

The bosses Henry in the Peach Bar and Kevin in the Lotus Club also maintain good relationships with the gangsters and pimps who inhabit the area. It's a means of protection as well as of keeping things running smoothly. The staff members in the mid-tier and low-end bars also keep a close eye on the police, who often let them know in advance when they have to implement the routine Yellow Crackdowns. The mid-tier bar owner rents an apartment near the bar and reserves it for his VIP clients. The apartment is a normal house, and the sex workers are the legal renters. Before the police arrive, the VIPs just go over to the apartment.

Maintaining VIP sex businesses that can accommodate large groups of men (usually from a company) as well as wealthier clients requires privacy, security, and upkeep; additionally, cleanliness is crucial for the clients to feel comfortable. This requires the collaboration of several parties and stakeholders. Wangkai said that he has rented the house for his own private group sex party and enjoyed a collaborative relationship with the mid-tier boss, Kevin, and the staff, pimps, and gangsters. Wangkai says:

> When the boss from the Peach Bar can arrange a VIP room for me and arrange a beauty queen for me, I feel very honoured and pleased! What a real man wants is a pretty and spicy bar girl! I can own a beautiful bar girl by using my own money and connection. I am very proud of myself that I have ability to collaborate and connect with influential people. I am a man among men!
>
> (Wangkai, 32)

Jianhuan agreed with what Wangkai said. When he gave money to the boss in the Peach Bar, he quickly got a table and sat with the prettiest sex workers available. He told me that he felt proud when he could maintain a good relationship with the boss of the Lotus Club. He was very assertive in telling me that he was a real man because he could afford to pay for the VIP room.

> It is amazing I could be arranged to a VIP room to avoid the tracking and crackdown from the police. It is an honour and definitely a status for me! I feel manly and masculine! Collaboration with the boss, police, and gangster makes me feel special and manly.
>
> (Jianhuan, 28)

What is frequently overlooked in sex work scholarship are the ways in which male purchasers of sex are also the ones selling the services of women to other men. However, money is crucial to avoid run-ins with the law. Bribes are needed to secure whole floors at upscale hotels or houses to keep away unwanted company and visits from policemen.

Male owners, gang members, hotel employees, and policemen collectively take advantage of and reproduce a patriarchal structure. This structure allows them to use women's sexual labour to negotiate and collaborate with each other, thereby asserting a masculinity defined more by exclusive homosocial bonds than by a competitive hierarchy.

Kevin says that he enjoys a good relationship with the agent who provides high-quality sex workers to them. He describes his network matter-of-factly:

> I have to pay the police. I have to get good connections with the police, gangsters, pimps, and clients. Sometimes I have to provide high-quality girls to the police for free. The police will give our VIP clients face and won't give them trouble. This is how collaboration works with different parties ...
>
> (Kevin, 35)

The other way that Kevin and Henry protect themselves is by using a dependable sex worker who pretends to own the bar. They have appointed two sex workers to manage their bar, which allows them to do things behind the scenes. To work with men of other professions and establish a network of male interdependency, Kevin uses patriarchal sexual relations between women and men, providing men with girls they have "tested" for quality at a discounted price. This reveals an obvious hypocrisy in the light of the state-mandated criminalization of sex sellers and purchasers, as many of these establishments rely on the cooperation of policemen and the purchasing power of wealthy government workers. Henry also has to cooperate with and offer higher salaries to sex workers if he wants a more innocuous cover for the business, and this reliance and mutual dependency mitigates an otherwise starkly uneven power relationship. For example, known connections with local gang members scare away most attempts by male clients to steal from the bar or become aggressive with sex workers. Additionally, the owners have a zero-tolerance policy for unsafe sex. This policy maintains an atmosphere of cleanliness and respectability. By collaborating with pimps, gangsters, and the boss of each niche market, the clients can enjoy the new type of collaborative masculinity.

Conclusion

Male migrants face multiple forms of emasculation that shape how they conceptualize and approach their sexual identities and sexual practices. As men, they are expected to secure well-paid jobs and be filial sons, which entails forming a family to extend their family bloodline. The demands of interpersonal relationships with their families and female peers and the societal expectation of marriage operate as day-to-day points of stress that lead many migrant men to feel as if their claim to desirable heterosexual manhood is contingent. Beyond their interpersonal and social lives, their status as factory migrants aggravates their sense of emasculation. Owing to the precarious nature of the employment, these men channel their heteronormative masculinity through purchased sex. Given their limited access to economic capital and their lack of upward career and economic mobility, my research reflects that within both the micro-environments of factory spaces and the macro-context of a contemporary China, these men face expectations that complicate their ability to perform a seemingly acceptable and desirable form of heteronormative masculinity.

As a result of navigating complex and competing discourses of male identity, these men adapt their sexuality and sexual needs distinctly. The chapter highlights how positionality and circumstances impact migrant men's views of masculinity. Dominant discourses surrounding masculinity may motivate particular sexual behaviour and lead men to understand their sexuality in a highly essentialist way. Entanglement provides a new perspective in understanding how masculinities and desires are differentially articulated and shaped by external economic, institutional, and demographic changes impacted by heteronormative expectations. Hence, the single-adult migrants generate different phantasms of masculinities that intersect with their major "entangled" life tensions. Some men embody vigorous and macho masculine identities to affirm their proximity to hegemonic masculinity. Others draw upon fantasy and bounded masculinity to engage in fantasy-oriented intimacy with sex workers. Some men engage in anxious and suppressive masculinity through rough sex and sadomasochism. Some migrant men use extravagant and competitive masculinity even though their salaries are not high. Finally, bragging and collaborative masculinity enables clients who collaborate with bosses, police, pimps, staff, and gangsters to enhance their masculinity. These men admitted that the encounters with sex workers allow them to experiment with explicit and performative feelings and understandings of power.

This research provides insight into how migrant men engage sex workers as an opportunity to negotiate their own anxieties and points of stress that relate to their masculinity and normative male sexuality. Popular discourse suggests that clients who buy commercial sex are lascivious and socially or morally deviant. This is especially true for single-adult migrants who are excluded from the marriage market because of their age, menial jobs, unattractive looks, and meagre incomes. These migrants face the psychosocial and emotional challenges that come with migration. These insights can help policymakers to decide how to provide retraining to the single-adult migrants and improve their working situation. This can provide time for the migrants to find a respectable partner and encourage them to get married. Subsequently, they will no longer pose a threat to society or participate in violence or disorder and so affect China's stability and harmony. Further research that contributes to improving knowledge about the commercial sex industry is crucial. Effective regulatory policy is needed to root out exploitation, sexual violence, and coercion.

PART THREE

Intimacy and Masculinity in High-End Niche Markets

levels of global service industry

codres

guanxi ⊖ elite social networks

[face] ⊖ emotional, relational labour

networks ⊖ capital $

entanglements ⊖ edgework

social reproduction

masculinities

exceptions

expressive emotional labour
from Fordist shap'g of worker to this
bounded authenticity? trad nanny

body capital

consumption / desire / neoliberalism

Stry Dogs
entangled masculing
rhizomatic relations
inter - Asia referencing
specos of cosmopolitanism
tourism

Reframing Love with a "Dirty Girl": High-End Sex Work and Intimate Relations in Urban China

As I walked around outside the Dragon Palace, I noticed that the well-known "gentlemen's club" was prominently located in a respected commercial centre of Dongguan. It is surrounded by other reputable restaurants and bars that are very popular at night. The hotel concourse is filled with European statues and paintings and lit with a luxurious chandelier. As I began my shift at the bar, the whole venue made me feel important, that what I did mattered.

Later that night I met Phoebe at the main bar in the Dragon Palace while she was waiting for her client. She had some time to sit and chat, so I handed her a Bloody Mary and let her begin. Phoebe was a typical Guangdong girl, tall, slim, with a good figure, long, silky black hair, and a naturally white skin. She was sporting a new out-fit, a one piece super-long cut dress to go with five-inch high heels and well-groomed vibrant red nails. She graduated from a business school in Guangdong but really wanted to earn easy money, meet foreigners, and relocate overseas. Her parents are entrepreneurs and they collude with cadres and professionals in China to make lucrative business deals. She did not like the atmosphere in her family and did not really want to follow her parents as a businesswoman. She earned around 50,000 yuan per month, excluding the money she had to give to the Dragon Palace. She worked only about 10 days per month. To her the job was quite relaxing and even fun. Clients were obsessed with her and they treated her like a princess. When asked about the likelihood of developing an intimate relationship with a client, she acknowledged the possibility. The clients in the Dragon Palace are well-off financially. The Dragon Palace charges a minimum of 1,000 yuan (US$150) per table to chat and drink with the girls. Typically these clients are managers of corporations, business owners, or even cadre members. Phoebe knew that any of them could take care of her financially:

> I am happy to talk to my clients online … I feel like I am searching for my boyfriend rather than just working in a bar. I love this feeling and treat my job as a *normal job* [author emphasis] with passion and pleasure …
>
> (Phoebe, 21)

The Dragon Palace is emblematic of a bourgeoning niche nightlife culture that caters to the rapid influx of business professionals and high-income earners, some of whom reside in Dongguan permanently and many of whom travel to Dongguan for business. Despite Phoebe's glamorous attire, many of the girls came to work wearing tight denim shorts that revealed clean-shaven legs. Their faces were made up to accentuate youthfulness, and they adorned themselves with fashionable jewellery.

They were uniformly young and come from relatively well-to-do families; many had obtained post-secondary education. Owing to their social positioning and the income they procured from working at the Dragon Palace, these women had unique economic resources at their disposal and access to elite social networks. As a result, many of the women interviewed viewed their work positively; these high-end bar girls generally enjoy the "financial, social, and emotional wherewithal to structure their work largely in ways that suited them and provided the ability to maintain healthy self-images" (Lucas, 2005, p. 541). Moreover, this assertion is substantiated by the socio-economic and cultural context of a post-reform China, wherein material possessions and patterns of consumption have, arguably, displaced political symbols as prominent indicators of social status (Yan, 2009, p. 208). The boss, Ken, left nothing to chance and provided female employees with training on appropriate ways of sitting, drinking, singing, dancing, and negotiating terms for sex. The Dragon Palace even hired a native English instructor to teach the "girls" English. It is essential for the bar's managers to maintain a friendly and close relationship with local cadres, which have the power to enforce (or to refuse to enforce) state regulations regarding the licensing and running of such businesses.

Because relational intimacy is more visible in the high-end market than in the others, its importance for understanding social character is more vividly manifested.[1] I argue that intimacy is always relational in

---

1 Before I begin with my analysis of the high-end commercial sex industry in China, I must first acknowledge that relational intimacy exists not only in the high-end market but also among some middle-tier sex workers, as illustrated by Choi and Holyroyd (2007).

nature. This chapter draws from several relevant perspectives, including Bourdieu's theories of economic capital and cultural capital (Bourdieu, 1984, 1986), Hochschild's (2003) theory of emotional labour, and
Bernstein's (2007) concept of bounded authenticity. Other important
insights come from recent work on individualization (Hansen, 2014;
Kipnis, 2012; Yan, 2010). I will explore below how high-end sex workers
incorporate the cultural concept of "face" to undertake a critical examination of emotional labour and capital in urban China. This chapter
illustrates how high-end sex workers' cultivation of long-term intimate
relationships with clients is a typical example of relational intimacy in
the commercial sex market.

Though (Hoang, 2014b) is discussing Vietnam, it is important to
understand the social character of gender through a relational approach
between sex workers and their clients in the Chinese context. China and
Vietnam share similar cultural histories as post-socialist countries, and
their sex industries are comparable. Both countries suffered through the
global financial crisis, and while China was the first developing country
in Asia to recover, Vietnam recovered quickly as well.

Some male customers in this context seek out and pursue an authentic emotional and sexual encounter. Both high-end sex workers and
their clients are "active social agents" who seek intimacy; some of them
go beyond paid intimacy to develop a genuine intimacy, which can lead
to mutual emotional support, monogamous dating, and even marriage.

Relational Intimacy in Boyfriend-Girlfriend Relationships in the West and South-East Asia

There is a growing body of literature on sex workers in China, the
West, and South-East Asia which looks to help us better understand
the unique experiences and common features between sex workers and
prostitutes in post-socialist China as well as other countries (Zheng,
2003, 2008, 2009; Otis, 2011; Liu, 2012).

There is less discussion about the complexity of the relational intimacy
between the parties involved (Zelizer, 2005). Nevertheless, entrepreneurial masculinity is a highly controversial notion, as it is implausible
to attribute men's need to live up to a modern entrepreneurial masculine image as a reflection of their resistance to state socialism. In her 2009
work, Zheng focused on local Chinese men in Dalian and seemed to
focus exclusively on a particular context between clients and sex workers (Zheng, 2009). Her narrative of a "coarsening of masculine identity"
may be specific to the low-end clients in the sex industry. More study
is needed to identify the nuances differentiating Chinese male clientele.

Jankowiak and Paladino (2008) in their introduction made a similar cross-cultural observation on how emotional bonding or intimacy can emerge out of an overt sexual situation.

The phenomenon of intimacy between sex workers and their clients is not exclusive to China; similar relationships have been identified in the West as well as in South-East Asia. Why do some males in the West, South-East Asia, and urban China develop intimacy with sex workers? Some evidence suggests that the relationship between clients (business elites and foreigners) and high-end sex workers involves greater emotional labour and intimacy than one finds among rural Chinese male clients. In the West and South-East Asia, it may be termed the "girlfriend experience." Here, what is sold is manufactured authenticity, whereby the sex worker acts as a girlfriend to meet the client's genuine desire for a real and reciprocal (albeit delimited sexual) connection (Bernstein, 2007; Brennan, 2004; Frank, 1998). This gender-as-relational approach (Bernstein, 2007; Frank, 1998, 2013) examines how the formation of intimacy within sex work is contingent upon the interplay of the socio-economic positioning of worker and client, the strategic performance of heteronormative gender, and the particular labour conditions that sex workers navigate. The relationship between high-end sex workers and clients involves emotional authenticity, which is explicitly brought into the economic contract.

In her pioneering studies of intimacy in sex work in Western societies, Bernstein observed that the relationships between lower-class streetwalkers and their clients involved direct exchanges of sex for money, whereas higher-class sex workers provided their clients with experiences of "bounded authenticity" (Bernstein, 2007). Her research indicates that upscale sex work requires greater emotional labour in order to generate an "authentic" experience, and that male clients in post-industrial societies seek various types of these sex exchanges.

The blurring of boundaries between commercial sex, love, and open relationships between local sex workers and foreign men is not uncommon in South-East Asia (Askew, 2002; Cohen, 1986; Cressy, 2008). Hamilton has examined the relationships between professional girls and *farangs* (foreigners) who became "boyfriends" rather than "clients" (Hamilton, 1997). She observed that some professional girls were able to form long-lasting emotional attachments with clients, even though the relationship was initially transactional and only for physical reasons. Hoang, examining the Vietnamese situation, found that high-end sex workers had the economic resources and social networks necessary to adopt some of the most expensive technologies of embodiment available in Ho Chi Minh City, such as plastic surgery (Hoang, 2010, 2011,

2014a). These women were looking for short- and long-term relationships with their clients, who included both overseas Vietnamese men and foreigners. Hoefinger has investigated how sex workers in Phnom Penh, Cambodia, used their linguistic abilities, cosmopolitan personas, and interpersonal skills to ascend the economic ladder and find enjoyment and professional satisfaction through their work (Hoefinger, 2011, 2013). In Cohen's study of the intimacy between Thai bar girls and foreign clients, who often only stay a short time in that country, he found that all of the clients came from anglophone countries (Cohen, 1986). By reviewing the "scribes" (letters) between the foreigners and their Thai girlfriends, Cohen discovered a connection in the relationships between "intimacy at a distance" and money. Although the foreigners were plagued by doubts over the seriousness, sincerity, and faithfulness of their Thai girlfriends, their relationships could not be reduced to the simple sexual exploitation of women because some eventually developed into permanent relationships.

These studies confirm that there are probably similar dynamics at work in China between sex workers and their clients. Perhaps there is a post-industrial sex work industry emerging in some of China's most developed cities that enables an intermingling of emotional labour, money, and intimacy to take place between sex workers and their clients. A sociocultural perspective involving economic and cultural capital, emotional labour, and bounded authenticity as a conceptual framework helps provide a clearer picture of the intimacy that develops between high-end sex workers and their clients.

In this chapter, I conceptualize economic and cultural capital, emotional labour, and bounded authenticity to describe the intimacy between sex workers and clients in the Dragon Palace. However, to fully understand the concept of intimacy between sex workers and clients, I add the cultural concept of "face" and apply it to examine China's commercial sex industry. The concept of face augments our understanding of what social scientists need to consider when interpreting both emotional labour and capital in urban China. While individualization and face are not the main concepts being examined here, the pursuit of individualization through commercialization has permeated the statements of several of the high-end sex workers interviewed.

Economic and Cultural Capital

The term "economic capital" is defined as the monetary income, assets, or other financial resources available for an individual to access (Bourdieu, 1986). "Cultural capital" refers to an actor's non-economic assets that help promote his/her upward social mobility (Bourdieu, 1984). These assets are normally acquired via the educational system and expressed as educational credentials, skills and knowledge, manners, lifestyles, and the associated consumption patterns. Both economic and cultural capital reflect the ability to acquire and manipulate a system of embodied, linguistic, and economic markets that carry cultural meaning, especially within a social status hierarchy (Bourdieu, 1977).

Emotional Labour

Hochschild's theory of emotional labour provides a foundation for comparing and understanding sex worker–client relationships in China (Hochschild, 2003/1983). According to Hochschild, emotional labour is "the management of feeling to create a publicly observable facial and bodily display" in addition to the labour that is "sold for a wage and therefore has exchange value" (Hochschild, 1983, p. 7). Many service professions require emotional labour.[2] Countless retail, entertainment, travel, hospitality, and related businesses expect employees to manage their feelings when dealing with their clients. The commonly held "customer is always right" adage reflects the importance of customer satisfaction to most businesses. Modern high-end sex work seems to have adopted the same perspective. Having undergone training programs provided by their employers, employees now consciously engage in evoking, shaping, or suppressing their feelings by changing their thoughts, physical conditions, and expressive gestures through both private superficial and deeper intrinsic acting exercises. In this context, it is important to examine how emotional labour varies between high-end and low-end sex services. The contention of emotional labour is that sex workers' expressed emotions, as a purchasable commodity, may be estranged from their true feelings, owing to the commercialization of their emotional displays. There is continuing debate as to whether intimacy between sex workers and their clients can be genuine or whether it is mostly a false sense of closeness induced by emotional labour.

---

2 Based upon her ethnographical study of American flight attendants and bill collectors, Hochschild understands emotional labour to be the commodification of private emotions sold for a profit in a capitalistic economy (Hochschild 2003/1983). Emotional labour varies by gender and social class, and women have far less independent access to money, power, authority, or status in society

Bounded Authenticity

Bernstein's notion of bounded authenticity draws attention to the question of whether intimacy between sex workers and their clients involves genuine emotional sharing, even though it is limited by time and coloured by the exchange of money (Bernstein, 2007). While her work identifies more positive experiences for upscale sex workers than many other accounts, she still offers the caveat that the exchange of money can only create limited intimacy.[3]

Capital, Selling Emotional Labour, and Individualization

High-end sex workers capitalize on their economic and cultural capital and use emotional labour to engage in long-term intimate relationships with their clients (Hoang, 2010, 2011). Today's sex workers have learned to embrace technology to promote and build their capital. They have adopted a variety of mobile telephone apps in order to promote themselves and extend the scope of their businesses (Hoang, 2014a).

High-end workers often have a higher level of cultural capital than their low-end counterparts. They typically have a post-secondary education, a basic level of conversational English, and the economic capital necessary to use technologies of embodiment (Foucault, 1988). As Hoang also observes, many sex workers alter their bodies to fit their clients' particular demands because their success depends upon the complete package of sexual attractiveness (Hoang, 2014a). The women interviewed acknowledge that they work to maximize verbal and non-verbal presentation skills. They exercise to hone their muscle tone and body shape and are meticulous in maintaining their hairstyles and make-up. Part of the regular routine is to assess facial features (full lips, long lashes, eye shape) and practise facial expressions and other non-verbal communication skills (emotional expressions, gestures, poses).

---

3 Bernstein (2007) contends that this "bounded authenticity" differentiates streetwalkers from the predominately middle-class, indoor sex workers in post-industrial societies. By "bounded authenticity," she means that the sale and purchase of sexual services does involve genuine emotional intimacy, albeit limited by time as well as by the fact that money is attached to the intimacy. Her study of high-end sex workers in San Francisco revealed that these women demanded exclusive privacy and performed repressive emotional labour in the form of suppressing their emotions of disgust towards their clients' bodies and ages. Bernstein's research indicates that there may be a transition from paid intimacy to full-fledged authentic intimacy between sex workers and their clients.

They also spend a lot of time and effort on verbal communication – flirting – skills (i.e., playfulness and paying attention to the personal needs of their clients). All this is in addition to the expectations about sexually oriented self-presentation and strategic considerations about how to maximize their potential body capital through means such as cosmetic surgery.

Playfulness and interpersonal dialogue are part of what makes a dating relationship appear "normal." The women interviewed routinely serve as "professional girlfriends" for their clients. From talking with them, it is evident that they also earn money by acting as long-term sexual companions to wealthy and socially prestigious men. At the top-end niche market that caters to local elite Chinese businessmen and foreigners, most of the sex workers speak English well and use plastic surgery and stylish clothing to maximize their attractiveness. The highest-paid sex workers are likely to have their own business and see themselves as cosmopolitan in outlook and lifestyle. In the current economic climate of post-reform Chinese society, those with money receive the most respect and prestige.

The following comments from interviewees give an indication of motivations.

> I come from a middle-class family. When I finished my degree in Guangzhou, I had no idea what kind of job I wanted. I hated office work and the civil service. I wanted to do something fun and interesting because I didn't need to take care of my parents ... I wanted to know more foreigners and extend my *guanxi* [social capital] to know more business elites. Then I worked in a bar as a bartender and I loved meeting foreigners. I find that foreigners are interesting, funny, and have a high sense of humour.
>
> (Phoebe, 21)

> I need money to enjoy life but I can work at something that is fun like meeting people, travelling, and going to different places. I don't have financial burdens like feeding parents or paying mortgages. I follow my heart to live.
>
> (Feifei, 23)

Cherry told me how she has to look in order to attract local businessmen and foreigners:

> For fashion, I try to look more modern and cosmopolitan to let my customers know I am worth what they pay. It doesn't cost me a lot of money

but I need attractive accessories so I can have the modern and cosmopolitan outlook and style.

(Cherry, 24)

Not surprisingly, the women who spend the most to portray themselves as highly fashionable also expressly desire upward mobility. They actively seek to secure their economic futures through individualism. Jess told me that she liked being in control and able to make decisions about her life. She could buy whatever she liked and did not need to earn the money to take care of her parents. She enjoyed her independence, which meant that she could control her own life by earning more money, and she had the autonomy to decide what she wanted to do with her life. She neither disregarded her parents' views about respectability nor disobeyed their wishes, since she did not need to support them.

The women interviewed all said that they were open to develop longer-term intimate relationships with their clients. They admitted that they used their work to increase their choices and preserve their financial futures. Most high-end sex workers know how to increase their earnings through self-improvement. They read online newspapers on their smartphones each day. They also watch news programs, listen to the radio, and read magazines to keep up on current affairs. They learn how to cook, and compare notes on how to understand men's emotions and personalities. This form of expressive emotional labour is used in hopes of possibly winning the heart of a client, which can enable them to enjoy an intimate and non-remunerative relationship (Hochschild, 2003/1983; Hoang, 2011). Fearful that their clients will one day become bored with their beauty, these women admitted that they work at keeping their regular customers by connecting with them and maintaining a kind of reciprocal intimacy via expressive emotional labour (Hoang, 2011). For example, the woman will remember specific clients' birthdays, favourite foods (and cook homemade meals, soups, or desserts, etc.), hobbies, and interests. Sex workers also buy food or gifts for their regular clients. They win the hearts of their clients by adopting this kind of "selling sex: selling heart" strategy (Hochschild, 2003/1983). For this type of sex work, the women are not only looking for money but also emotional involvement and intimacy (Zelizer, 2005).

In 2007, Chelsea (25) was just an 18-year-old greeter at a club in Dongguan. She would greet the clients coming in and check the time and with whom they had made the appointment. Clients who arrived on time were given the best seats. Those who arrived late were seated in less desirable areas at the club. Chelsea found she had a natural talent for networking and connecting with clients. In less than a year, a manager asked her if she would like to become a "mommy" ("madam" or sex work manager). In the beginning, Chelsea had only four sex workers; two were from the company and two were her own friends. But in only one month, the number of workers she managed grew to 20 in total. Three years later, she proudly told me that she had 200 sex workers under her management in the Dragon Palace. She said "You are the workers' mommy but also the clients' mommy."

Giving face to clients is an important form of emotional labour. Chelsea said she knows how to enhance "face" and trust in public for clients. She taught her girls the skills of managing their behaviour to make the clients appear strong and sexy as well as making them feel they are the envy of other men. For example, the girls are taught that they need to look elegant, but with undertones of sexiness. They are taught to speak clearly and with eloquence. They must also act appropriately so that the client looks strong, successful, and in control when meeting at the club with other business associates. Chelsea describes her service as a combination of physical and emotional labour. Sometimes, bar girls use their own social networks with other local rich men and even cadres to help their clients run their businesses. This is how the girls and the club enhance the client's "face" and further build up relations of "trust" with people across business sectors. In the Dragon Palace, sex workers engage in expressive emotional labour and relational work as reflected in mutual intimacy and relationship building with their clients. As such, high-end sex workers view their relationships with clients within the rhetoric of love and emotional attachment. Their notions of love are integrated with needs, materiality, and economic pragmatism.

Most of the high-end sex workers interviewed in Dongguan capitalized on their cultural capital to cultivate intimacy and long-term relationships through mobile and online apps in order to generate more business with local elites, middle-class clients, or foreigners (Hoang, 2014a). For example, April disrobes for private audiences using WeChat, QQ, and Skype. Because she does not need to pay commission for her webcam performances, she can keep 100 per cent of her earnings and perform either at a karaoke lounge or even from home. Similarly, Elaine has created professional accounts on WeChat, QQ, WhatsApp, and Skype. She charges each of her clients (around 30 in total) a monthly subscription fee to chat with her via these accounts: her going rate is 300 yuan (US$48) for WeChat, QQ, and Weibo, and 400 yuan (US$65) for Skype. According to Elaine,

> Sometimes men ask for specific photos or videos. A set of 10 pictures can sell for 30 yuan [US$4] or 40 yuan [US$5] [in addition to the monthly fee]. But sometimes, I don't even have to be naked. As long as they are arous-

ing, I can send photos like taking a shower, wearing a high-slit dress to show my long and sexy legs, or wearing a bikini ... However, I would like to make it more like a friendship, because these customers coming back are more important than the money itself. If my clients like my photos, they will try to talk to me and we may go out on a date. Chatting online can give me a way to know more about the client and whether we have the potential to develop a relationship or not.

(Elaine, 21)

April's experiences were similar to Elaine's:

Since we talk through WeChat, we can have a better understanding of each other. Our friendship changes the relationship on both sides. It turns the client into a friend and even a short-term partner. Once our friendship is established, I'll become their girlfriend forever.

(April, 23)

Online connections with clients were also important to Phoebe:

This is my full-time job. I am happy I can talk to my clients online and get to know them better. I can carry on a conversation with my regular clients. Some men crave companionship, and they are the ones who tend to spend more money on me. I feel like I am searching for my boyfriend rather than just working at a job. I love this interactive relationship.

(Phoebe, 21)

Not only do messaging apps foster deeper and potentially more lucrative relationships, but they also enable the sex workers to be their own bosses. They can work full time in a karaoke lounge, then go directly to the client online, cutting out intermediaries and keeping all the income. With such cultural capital in hand, they can make full use of their bargaining powers to work towards the job they like, stay physically attractive with the technologies of embodiment, and use mobile apps to chat with foreigners and business elites online (Hoang, 2014b). Lisa Dalby's excellent 1990s book *Geisha* makes a similar observation in this respect. These all provide the means for workers to forge relationships with their clients. If they feel a spark or connection, they can try to develop bonds of emotional intimacy.

As the globalized and globalizing economic shift gathered momentum throughout the 1980s and 1990s, material possessions and patterns of consumption in China displaced political symbols of social status (Yan, 2009, p. 208). This has not only changed perceptions of the

individual but has also raised expectations for freedom, choice, and
individuality (Kipnis, 2012). The individual has also become a basic
social category in China, and this development has begun to perme-
ate all areas of social, economic, and political life (Hansen, 2014). Individualization and commercialization have been embraced by many sex
workers at the high end who were never the intended targets of the
state-sponsored program of individualization. Nevertheless, the desire
of these sex workers to pursue freedom from hardship via individualization in the sex industry stems from the mandated instrumentally
rational individualization (Yan, 2009). This provided the impetus for
the new bourgeoisie to consume, and even borrow, at the government's
behest, in order to buy more than they need (Yan, 2009). There is a clear
sense that the sex workers featured in this chapter are an unintended
consequence of contemporary macro-economic policy and its cultural
sequelae. The high-end sex workers devote a significant percentage of
their earnings to maintaining a conspicuously fashionable lifestyle even
as they seek to secure their emotional and economic futures. These sex
workers have the freedom to choose their own roles and identities as
they try to cultivate long-term relationships with their clients.

Bounded Authenticity, Intimacy, and Face

The second focus for this chapter is on how clients overcome barriers to
develop such relationships with sex workers in the Dragon Palace. According to Goffman, both Chinese and foreigners are concerned with "face" in
the sense of pride, honour, and dignity (Goffman, 1972). However, owing
to cultural differences in how this concern with face plays out, there are
different considerations for Chinese and foreign men within the particular
context of marriage with a sex worker. It is important to note that typically
these clients do not perceive the women to be cheap, dirty, or vulgar.

In Dongguan, most of the clients who agreed to participate in an interview were foreigners, vacationers, overseas Chinese, or local business
elites staying in the city either temporarily or permanently. A significant
number were divorced men aged between 30 and 60. They tended to look
for partners who had a sense of humour, were not "cheap," and knew how
to enjoy life and enjoy the bedroom. Reciprocity is important. Women willing to buy drinks for their clients will in return have drinks, cigarettes, and
meals purchased for them. Although many local women hope for love,
they will settle for material recognition and future security, usually in the
form of marriage. Some clients admitted that they liked to consort with
multiple professional girls at the same time, just as a girl may also serve
several clients until she finds one with whom she feels she can connect.

Goffman remarked that face is universal, for people everywhere are the same (Goffman, 1972, p. 44). Face is not an exclusively Chinese phenomenon: "concern for face is not solely an 'Asian' phenomenon, but rather it is found in individuals from all societies and ethnic groups" (Lau & Wong, 2008, p. 52), and the social necessity to orient oneself to one's own public self-image or face during interactions is universal (Brown & Levinson, 1987, p. 62). Individuals, irrespective of their cultural background, cannot disregard the opinions or appraisals of others in their own self-understanding.

Intimacy between Sex Workers and Non-Chinese Clients

The Dragon Palace has so many workers that they need several mommies. I met one of them, Margaret, in 2016. She says, "I did not want to force anything until I met my *laowai* [foreign] boyfriend Benedict." Benedict came from England, and she says he gives her a sense of security and he doesn't mind her past. They were living together and had plans to marry, but had not done so at the time of the interview. Margaret says,

> I guess we are just going with the flow, when we both want to get married then we will. I've already been married once, as long as I'm happy with him I don't really care.
>
> (Margaret, 21)

Benedict doesn't have much money, but she says he's an honest guy and he doesn't mind that Margaret is a sex worker. He also knows that Margaret works in a bar as a mommy. He is doing business in China and Margaret has a lot of connections, so she sometimes recommends someone his company might do business with. She also taught him to speak Chinese (Putonghua). In fact, sometimes she pays for his meals.

Another couple that emerged was Kim and Michael. Michael, a 45-year-old American professional, went to Dongguan in 2001 to work for one of the multinational enterprises. Kim worked in one of the bars, and in the beginning, Michael met her strictly for sex. They initially communicated through WeChat, but later engaged in non-transactional, non-remunerative sex, which evolved into deeper feelings of love and affection. They each continued to engage with multiple sex partners even as their commitment to one another grew. Finally, they agreed to get married. After getting married, Michael bought Kim a house and helped her set up a business in Dongguan:

> After meeting Michael, we developed more than a client-customer relationship. He bought my services in the beginning, and we chatted through

WeChat and exchanged some photos of each other. I think I was hunting for a boyfriend rather than just working in a karaoke lounge. After our souls connected, we knew we loved each other and he became my long-term partner. We are well connected and have developed some form of chemistry.

(Kim, 24)

Coming from America, Michael was not embarrassed to introduce his wife to his friends and family, nor did he feel ashamed or experience a loss of face by having a wife with a history in the sex industry. In interviews, it was clear that he believed Kim genuinely liked or loved him. By comparison, he claimed that his ex-wife was unattractive, domineering, and rude to him. He loves narrow eyes and long black hair. However, he did admit that he is plagued by doubts as to Kim's seriousness, sincerity, and faithfulness. Michael told me:

It's not like what people think. She's not a bad or dirty girl even though she works in a bar. She is interesting and knows how to enjoy life. She knows how to run a business and she's got a lot of social network connections in China … I was divorced twice and I feel like I finally found a girl who can understand me. She's beautiful and petite and someone I want to have a family with. Most important, we have chemistry, and that to me is love. I don't hide her past from my family. It is nothing to be ashamed of.

(Michael, 45)

I interviewed Bill and Huang at an expensive bar in Dongguan. Bill, a British national, met Huang (24) in 2004. At the time of the interview, they were not yet married but had been together for four years. Bill said that in the beginning he was attracted by Huang's talents and cosmopolitan appearance. He was unhappily married at the time, and soon after divorced his wife. By comparison, Bill said, Huang is modern and sophisticated but really needs a man to take care of her. Huang now has her own business in Dongguan. Bill described Huang:

Huang is a sensitive and gentle soul. That type of girl is perfect for someone like me. I want to take care of her and raise a family together… To me, marriage is finding the right person to make your life complete, meaningful, and fruitful… I honestly believe we are meant to be together.

(Bill, 49)

I asked Michael and Bill whether they lost face when they introduced their partners to their parents and friends:

Actually, I don't think I ever treated Kim like a sex worker in the beginning; I always just treated her like my girlfriend. All that bar-girl stuff is past tense, especially now that she has her own business. I don't think I ever felt ashamed about her past; not with my family or my friends anyhow. When they asked where we met, I told them we hooked up at a night club and the whole thing was really romantic… I was divorced before and I don't have anything to be ashamed of and neither does she.

(Michael, 45)

I think Huang is very well educated and speaks English very well. She has fun in her life. I treat her working at the bar as *only* [author's emphasis] a job. She is not dirty at all and I don't think I will lose face in front of my friends and relatives. She is very cosmopolitan and modern when we meet our friends. When I told my friend and parents she was working in a bar, they were not surprised at all. Face is not an issue for me in front of my family and circle of friends.

(Bill, 49)

In the interviews, many of the foreigners described Chinese girls as cute, slim, expressive, and caring. Most of the high-end girls are grateful for the attention these men give them. Their relatively small size and slight frames make the foreigners feel strong and gallant, evoking feelings of wanting to protect them. According to Michael, Kim's soft and enchanting voice will "make him dance." Michael accepts and desires the traditional gender stereotype that positions a wife as a nurturing helper and a man as the key provider.

Intimacy between Sex Workers and Chinese Clients

Zhu, a 40-year-old Chinese elite, always comes to the Dragon Palace to visit his professional cuties. He orders whisky at US$250 a bottle. Buying whisky situates Zhu with a degree of cultural capital. His sense of pride is also elevated when paying the bill for the evening. He beamed with pride when he told me he can spend up to US$5,000 per night, especially when he is with overseas business partners who insist on splitting the bill and paying with a credit card. This is laughable to Zhu, who always pays in cash. Zhu's behaviour is hardly unique. For Chinese businessmen it is through conspicuous consumption that their masculinity and their sense of "face" are articulated.

Moreover, as the norm, customers at the bar were expected to make grand gestures by purchasing expensive champagne or whisky. On one occasion, Peng, a tycoon in his mid-30s, ordered more than six bottles of Dom Perignon at US$557 a bottle. He insisted on Dom Perignon because it was the most expensive champagne at the bar. Notably, the minimum charge to get the table next to the prettiest girl was at least 3,100 yuan (US$500). It is through these displays of extravagance that most of the local Chinese convert economic capital to symbolic capital to perform a distinct form of masculinity.

Another example of an affluent businessman's motive for patronizing high-end venues can be found in Zheng's thoughts on high-end women. Originally from Zhejiang, he spent 10 years in Scotland, before marrying Sasa (21), whom he met at the gentlemen's club, in 2012. At the time of the interview, Sasa was no longer working in a bar and was instead running her own business in Dongguan. According to Zheng:

> She is just a little unlucky girl who got stuck in Dongguan. But I am so passionate about her since she is hot, cute, talented, smart, and has lots of business skills. I was divorced, and it took me 20 years to find my true love. She has never borrowed money or cheated on me. I know it is very difficult for you to understand, but I think it is chemistry and true love.
>
> (Zheng, 50)

Wang is an educated and wealthy Chinese businessman from Guangzhou. Divorced twice, he had had multiple partners before he met Ruby (22) at an expensive bar. After they fell in love with each other, Ruby left the bar to work in a computer company. They had been in a long-term relationship for five years in 2013:

> Before I met Ruby, I had multiple partners with some girls, single-parent women, and some married women. Everyone has a history. I don't think I am a dirty old man. You should not prejudge Ruby. She is a nice girl and I want to start a family with her. I can connect and communicate with Ruby and true love has no boundary.
>
> (Wang, 45)

When asked if they worried about losing face when they introduced their wives to their parents and friends, the men replied:

> It is not shameful at all. I don't care about face. All I care about is a life partner. It is too difficult to find a woman who can understand me. It took me 10 years to find my true love and we can connect. It is not easy to find a life partner and I cherish her a lot. Her past is history. Sex worker is only a job and it deserves more respect. Sasa is well educated and she liked working in a bar. Why do I think I will lose face?
>
> (Zheng, 50)

I will tell my parents Ruby was a bar girl but I never said she was a sex worker. Strictly speaking, she is not a sex worker. I don't need to publicly announce her job. What I care about is whether I have chemistry with Ruby and I am glad we found each other. True love, caring, intimacy is all I care about now. We have been together for nine years and she hasn't asked me for money.

(Wang, 45)

According to both Wang and Zheng, there is little shame in marrying a former high-end sex worker. They believe that they have established a form of intimacy and bounded authenticity between them. Most of the high-end sex workers are physically attractive and fashionable, knowledgeable about current affairs, and have some means or *guanxi* to do business in China. Working in a bar is perceived to be a normal job and has little stigma attached to it. The sale and purchase of sexual services involves genuine emotional intimacy, as suggested by Bernstein (2007). The enactment of friendship, mutual trust, and romance by many of these clients stands in stark contrast to the commonly cited image of sex work as "paid rape" (Sanders, 2008a). Within this particular context, sex workers and clients find some measure of intimacy, care, authenticity, and chemistry to create long-term and even marital relationships. Sanders also finds that male customers did not view sex workers "simply as bodies" or as "targets of sexual conquest" but instead as a meaningful, personal connection (Sanders, 2008b, p. 98). Bernstein describes "authentic (if fleeting) libidinal and emotional ties with clients, endowing them with a sense of desirability, esteem, or even love" (Bernstein, 2007, p. 103). In exchange, sex workers not only receive considerable material and financial rewards but may also achieve socio-economic advancement and find enjoyment in their lives.

The affluent overseas and upper-class Chinese men and foreigners alike are concerned with face, but the cultural differences in how this plays out lead to different considerations for Chinese and foreign men in marrying women who were employed as sex workers. Both foreigners and affluent Chinese men develop a high sense of bounded authenticity, relationship, and intimacy with the sex workers. The foreigners generally seek and construct a gender-normative marriage. They believe that the Chinese women hold these traditional values about marriage roles. With their attentive listening skills, appreciative laughter, and comments of affirmation, regardless of their authenticity, the sex workers perform expressive forms of emotion, which help the men to feel respected, admired, and masculine. The Chinese men focus on the bounded authenticity, intimacy, and chemistry that is generated from their relationship with the high-end sex workers. The relationship is more natural and does not involve acting, lies, or cheating.

Most of the research revealed that high-end and mid-tier sex workers may have a lower incidence of drug addiction (Oselin, 2009, 2010; Sanders, 2007) and fewer arrests (Cunningham & Kendall, 2011) than those at the low end. Prior research shows that exiting from sex work may not be a single, concrete event but rather a process. It may involve specific stages, such as preparing financially for exit, undergoing psychological therapy, reconciling with family, severing ties with industry friends, and/or receiving assistance with housing and vocational skill development (Månsson & Hedin, 1999; Sanders, 2007).

Longitudinal Data to Study Intimacy between Sex Workers and Clients

There is limited research regarding whether finding a relationship with a client can help a woman exit completely from the commercial sex industry. After I was familiar with the sex workers with whom I worked in the Dragon Palace, I kept communicating with some of them with WeChat or Skype. When I came back to China in the summer of 2016, most of the sex workers I had met in 2010 had either changed their jobs or married Chinese or foreigners. Some were still living in China and some had relocated overseas. I interviewed 20 couples who are now living in Hong Kong (6), London (4), Melbourne (4), Europe (3), and the US (3) by using telephone interviews in summer 2017. I met all of them in the Dragon Palace in 2013–16. Longitudinal data was collected by repeat interviews using the telephone as well as the WeChat app. These women spoke about how sex workers forged romantic relationship with their clients and got married, and how it helped them exit from the commercial sex industry. They were either becoming mothers or starting new jobs outside China. They all said that they enjoyed a good marriage and a happy family and living abroad. But they also admitted that they experienced a lot of pressure and problems related to this career change. Issues related to intimacy, chemistry, trust, and desires were ongoing struggles with their former client/husband.

These (former) sex workers perceived that there were opportunity costs involved in sex work, but the marriage had changed their life course and given their life a new meaning. Most of the 20 couples told me that they encountered many ups and downs. Kyla is a mother of three children and has her own restaurant in Florida. She recalled that at the very beginning when she married Donald (43), who is an American, she did not adapt well to her new life in the United States.

> I haven't adjusted well in [the US]. I lost my identity and it's very boring in the USA. With the love and care of Donald, he spends most of his time accompanying me. I tried to find something to do here. Since I am good at cooking, I opened a Chinese restaurant. At the beginning, we lost money and we owed a lot of debt to the bank. However, we are still making it, clearing out the debt … but I am happy I can have a new life …
>
> (Kyla, 23)

Carroll (37) and Ashley (22) are living in London now. They have a six-month-old daughter. Ashley comes from a well-to-do family and her dad is a cadre member in Chongqing. She found that at the beginning it was difficult to adjust to life in London. She says,

> When I married Carroll, we did not have too much in common. He is fine with my former job and did not mind what I did before. I started finding part-time work and tried to become a good wife for him. Then I realized that this is not something I could do. I could not even work as a receptionist or sales since the job was so demanding. Our lives seem a little bit better after I gave birth to our angel baby girl – Jade – in January [2017]. Carroll likes our angel a lot and our relationship is getting much better now.
>
> (Ashley, 22)

Ann (22) comes from Anhui. She married Scott (36), who is from Scotland. She invested her money in a beauty parlour in Guangzhou so that she could focus on the cosmetology business. However, Scott was afraid that Ann would fall back in with her so-called sisters from her sex work days, and he's afraid she cannot avoid the temptation to go back. Ann was popular as a sex worker and made a high income. After some time, Scott decided that his only option was to take Ann with him back to his hometown to start a new life. It was difficult for Scott to find a good job in Scotland, since all his professional networks were in China. However, Ann suggested running a new beauty parlour there. After drying up all their savings, Scott had to get a business loan from the local bank. They struggled to make the loan payments each month. At the beginning, business was so bad that Scott began drinking heavily. One night he lost his temper and beat her. Ann had to go to a women's shelter to escape. She eventually got Scott into counselling, and business at the beauty parlour improved. At last report, the parlour has 30 staff and the business is making a profit. At home, they are raising their infant son.

Women such as Ann, Ashley, and Kyla represent sex workers who have financial and personal security that renders sex work almost as a hobby to them. They are motivated by the familiarity that they have with Dongguan's commercial sex industry and the particular circles of sex workers and clients whom they worked with when they were younger. Their experience reveals that access to financial and personal security does not ensure that women will never return to the commercial sex industry. Most of them encountered intercultural struggles and social network problems, and lost their identity by moving far away from their earlier life. However, with the chemistry and love cultivated with their former clients, they tried to start a new life. Forging a relationship with a former client might play well in popular films, but the actual struggles are cautionary tales about the psychological scars and ongoing temptation to return to the commercial sex industry.

Conclusion

This chapter examined the expectations and roles of high-end sex workers in the Dragon Palace and how relationships evolved with some of their clients. It focused on two research questions. The first question was to explore how high-end sex workers mobilize their economic and cultural capital to seek long-term intimate relationships with their clients. Similar to the subjects in Hoang's findings, these high-end sex workers make the most of their advantages in economic capital, cultural capital, and emotional labour to engage with more affluent clients (Hoang, 2010, 2011). The sex workers provide emotional labour, which is the commodification of private emotions intended to be sold for a profit in a capitalist economy (Bernstein, 2007). High-end sex workers also take advantage of technologies of embodiment to transform or manipulate their bodies in order to maximize their physical beauty and attractiveness (Hoang, 2014a). We found that high-end sex workers and their clients routinely engage in both pecuniary transactions and also genuine intimate and non-remunerative exchanges.

The second question in this chapter was to investigate how clients overcome social stigma to develop such relationships with sex workers. Through interviews, these "professional cuties" and "sweethearts" make their own choices and negotiate structural inequalities with fortitude and ingenuity, finding satisfaction in both their work and their daily life. Both Chinese and foreign men have some concerns with face or reputation regarding a committed relationship with a sex worker, but they both develop a high sense of bounded authenticity, relationship, and intimacy. The foreigners generally construct and obtain a gender-normative marriage, while the overseas and affluent local Chinese men focus more on a bounded authenticity and non-remunerative relationship with the sex workers.

Chapter 5 will deal with concept of reciprocating desires between high-end sex workers and non-Chinese clients in the Dragon Palace. Reciprocating desire shapes how these workers and clients navigate intimacy and needs in post-socialist China.

Reciprocating Desires: The Pursuit of Desirable East Asian Femininity in China's High-End Commercial Sex Industry

May comes from Shandong and works in the high-end Dragon Palace. Inside this club, she is a superstar. Tall, thin, vivacious, and popular, she was always upbeat and positive. So it surprised me one day to see her upset as I was preparing drinks for some clients relaxing at the bar. It was the first time I'd seen her unhappy. She looked at me as if she wanted to talk, so I excused myself and walked over to her. We sat in a quiet corner and she lowered her voice to confide in me. She said,

> David said I have something special that makes me alluring. I have very long lashes and my eyes are watery so I look very bright. I don't need to say anything, I just need to stand there and men will fall for me. David is not as rich as Chinese, however, he is more polite and chivalrous. He promises me to take me to Los Angeles but I have to quit my current job. He wants me all to himself. So I am thinking, financially, he can't give me 100,000 yuan [US$16,129] each month but that's what I am making now. David is humorous, interesting and knows how to enjoy life. I struggle whether I shall quit my current job but I believe David is probably the once in a lifetime man. I think I will quit soon because money is not everything ...
>
> (May, 23)

May's story is typical of the high-end sex workers I interviewed in the Dragon Palace, which caters to both wealthy Chinese men and non-Chinese men. This chapter focuses on 50 non-Chinese clients who come from North America, Britain, and Europe and on 50 girls in the Dragon Palace. The relational ties between the workers and clients in mid- and low-tier bars are weak, and sex workers in these bars face day-to-day struggles and harassment that are accentuated by their class. Mid- and low-tier sex workers were explicit in stating that sex work was a preferred career move, given their alternatives in the formal labour sector, poorly paid and exhausting factory and service jobs. The decision to pursue sex work was a practical utilitarian step, given the personal financial obligations that these migrant peasant workers faced and sex work's considerable financial rewards (Tsang, 2017b). The clients in mid- and low-tier bars bought commercial sex for sexual satisfaction but not for desire (Tsang, 2017b). However, the general lack of enthusiasm that characterized low-tier sex workers was notably absent in the accounts of high-tier sex workers, who were comparatively more likely to discuss their work in a positive light.

In high-end bars, the relationships built between clients and workers are often more permanent and complex, which renders "desire" a topic worthy of exploration. Moreover, the economic impact of high-tier sex work is often highly nuanced. Sex workers in high-end bars actively contribute to China's economy by helping Chinese men obtain various kinds of economic capital. Sex workers bring in FDI (foreign direct investment) from men who commission sex work for business purposes and overseas remittances from men engaged in recreational sex (Xiao, 2011). Taking these factors into account, investigating bars frequented by non-Chinese men will cast light on the impact of globalization, economic reform, and political economy on China's sex industry. Therefore, this chapter mainly focuses on non-Chinese clients, excluding those who come from South-East Asia. Investigating bars frequented by Western men can cast light on the impact of globalization on China's sex industry. Generally it is no surprise that high-end sex workers have an advantage over low-end ones in their ability to develop long-term intimate relationships with foreigners in the commercial sex market (Tsang, 2017a). Both high-end sex workers and their clients are "active social agents" who seek intimacy and have the resources needed to be successful in this context (Tsang, 2017a).

This chapter examines how socio-economic conditions impact heteronormative sexual desires between high-end sex workers and their clients in urban South China. First, how do female Chinese sex workers in high-end bars engage their desires with clients through their body work and body capital? Second, why and how has China's post-socialist transition reshaped women's gender ideologies and contributed to a moral vacuum which is evidenced by sex work in high-end bars? Drawing from Hoang's (2015) interpretation of "dealing in desires" and Rofel's (2007) *Desiring China*, the chapter considers how desire circulates in high-end bars and its impact on how workers and clients negotiate their relationships. This chapter unfolds as a theoretical exercise in unearthing and understanding the underpinnings of how socio-economic contexts impact our understanding of what qualify as reciprocating desires.

In particular, the conditions and realities that sex workers and clients in urban China negotiate are recognized and discussed. The workers in the high-end bars see sex work as a means of pursuing their individualization, which reflects the nation's accelerated transition to a country of individualized desires.

Conceptual Tools for Understanding the Sociology of Desire

Some important studies help our understanding of intimacy between sex workers and clients (Bernstein, 2007; Frank, 2002; Hoang, 2015; Hoefinger, 2013; Rivers-Moore, 2016). For example, Allison (1994) reported that white-collar male Japanese clients (salarymen) pursued corporate masculinity in Tokyo nightclubs and were often open to developing intimacy with high-end sex workers. Bernstein (2007) found evidence of intimacy between the middle-class sex workers and clients in San Francisco, but that intimacy was constrained by bounded authenticity. Frank's (2002) work examined strip club regulars and the types of intimate relationships that can emerge over time. Work by Rivers-Moore (2016) found that young, attractive high-end sex workers in Costa Rica have been able to establish long-term intimate relationships with American clients.

There is also abundant literature regarding the importance of body work and body capital in sex work as well as other industries (Butler, 1993; Bernstein, 2008; Brents & Jackson, 2013; Rivers-Moore, 2013, 2016). For example, Butler (1993) mentioned how body capital and body work affect sexual activity and performance. Brents and Jackson (2013) identified that gender, emotional labour, and interactive body work were important in many different workplaces as well as in the sex work industry. Bernstein (2008) identified the importance of body capital in the high-end commercial sex industry in San Francisco. However, the discussion of dealing in desires in an Asian context, particularly in China, is limited. Following a more thorough examination of this literature, I can apply these insights to the Asian experience – drawing on Hoang (2015) and Rofel (2007) – to then discuss China in the modern context.

Hoang's (2015) framework in "dealing in desire" brings together two important theoretical insights. First, sexual desire is the proverbial "black box" at the core of every individual. Second, this desire can be applied to macro-social changes in a society like Vietnam. Taking these two points into consideration suggests that the acquisition of body capital satisfies desire while fuelling future desire. Sexual desire is not simply a physical craving, but is inextricably linked to self-esteem

acquisition of body capital

and sexual performance. Sexual performance and sexual app manipulated by technological embodiment – cosmetic surgery. Women transform or manipulate their bodies through particular procedures to attain a desired image of beauty, individualization, and cosmopolitan identity. Women who use their body work to access upward economic and social mobility are active agents who control their lives and career paths. "Body work" refers to modifications that individuals inflict on their own bodies or the bodies of others (Hoang, 2014a, p. 516). "Body capital" (Brents & Jackson, 2013; Bernstein, 2008; Wacquant, 1995) describes how the bodies that are worked on become valued in competitive consumer contexts (Hoang, 2014a, p. 516). Sex workers engage different technologies of embodiment to manipulate their bodies or alter their embodied performance of femininity so as to cater to the desires of their clients.

In *Desiring China*, Rofel (2007, p. 111) evokes cosmopolitanism and modernity. Rofel suggested that encompassing social structures impact lived experience and collective subjectivities, and shape individual identity to unearth power enacted by the universal pursuit of modernity. Rofel depicts young women in a post-socialist China expressing their newfound freedom and cosmopolitanism through the consumption of goods and services. Cosmopolitan identity holds particular significance within the context of China. Rofel (2007) says that the ideal Chinese citizens embody "cosmopolitanism with Chinese characteristics" to embrace knowledge, connect with their world, and rethink their identity (Rofel, 2007, p. 112). However, these Chinese individuals tend to situate their sense of "self" through their ability to accumulate social, economic, and cultural capital, which holds immeasurable importance in the construction of a desirable cosmopolitan identity.

Combining Hoang's and Rofel's respective frameworks leads by extension to "reciprocating desires" as a socially and collectively constructed process. The individuals use their own body capital to create intimate relationships that are embedded in a wider social, historical, economic, and cultural context in post-reform China.

Post-Socialist Transitions in China

The cultural significance of sex work in post-socialist China is but one of the many consequences of events leading up to and including the global financial crisis of 2008. At that time, China's economy was steadily rising, and society was focusing on conspicuous consumption and pursuing a materialistic quality of life. But after the financial crash,

tens of thousands of workers were suddenly displaced and left struggling to find any means to earn a living. The recession was especially
harsh on the vast numbers of young women who toiled in sweatshops.
Many came from rural areas before the crash, lured by the promise of
rising wages and steady employment. The crash led to hundreds of
sweatshops closing operations, forcing the women onto the streets. A
significant number found that sex work paid quickly and paid well. In
fact, sex work was far more lucrative and provided more benefits than
working in the factory (Tsang, 2017a, 2017b).

Desire in the sex trade is shaped by China's newly emerging emphasis on consumerism and individualism and is closely related to state
policy (Hoang, 2015; Tsang, 2014; Tsang et al., 2018; Tsang, 2019). Success
is widely measured by material possessions. For those in the sex work
industry, the money seems like a quick way to attain upward mobility
even though the work remains both socially unacceptable and illegal.
But China is undergoing major social changes and even this form of
deviance may be reframed. In the eyes of both clients and workers, it is
justified as a conduit through which new forms of social capital can be
acquired against the backdrop of ever-increasing consumerism practices.

China was one of the first Asian countries to rebound from the
2008 global economic crisis. Since then, China's consumer revolution
became even more robust than pre-2008. China's FDI and GDP have
grown steadily since then, with double-digit growth rates recorded in
2008, 2010, and 2011 (Davies, 2013). China-bound FDI increased from
US$92.4 billion in 2008 to US$117.2 in 2012. China's GDP increased by
7% over a single quarter in 2014 (Davies, 2013).

As mentioned earlier, after losing their jobs in sweatshops, women
found they could earn ten, twenty, even one hundred times as much
money as sex workers. The changing structure, economy, and culture
in post-reform China has focused almost entirely on equating success
with economic gain. But the avoidance of political, religious, or ethical
perspectives has created a "value vacuum" (Link, Madsen, & Pickowicz, 2013). The term "moral vacuum" or "value vacuum" means that, in
the post-reform era, following the collapse of a strong public ideology,
a uniform moral ideology is lacking (Link et al., 2013). In the absence
of activism based on values or morals, China promotes economic gain
and individual success. If the primary measure of success is upward
mobility, it is not surprising that many sex workers find solace and jus-
tification within this context.

Within the context of this growing consumer revolution, China's
hyper-materialism has melded with the re-evaluation of sexual norms
to create conditions that make sex work socially acceptable or even

desirable among the well-to-do sex workers found in places like the Dragon Palace. China's post-socialist transition has reshaped women's gender ideologies. Kavanaugh (2015) identified the masculinity crisis as related to structural changes and cultural context. Therefore, sex workers in both high-end and low-end bars follow the Chinese policy of pursuing moneymaking. Moneymaking has filled the space to become the most conspicuous public value and has been internalized in the individual's everyday life practice. Getting rich remains the dominant value in China, and many are seeking to take advantage of the changing times. With the emphasis on economic gain and the absence of moral ideologies in post-socialist China, women have found that sex work provides them opportunity and rewards that eluded them in the factory. Both high-end and low-end bar girls capitalize their own body capital to deal with desires as they negotiate client relationships.

Reciprocating Desires between Sex Workers and Clients in a High-End Bar

Desire is a fluid concept with varied meanings. For the high-end sex workers interviewed, desires with regard to clients hinged upon becoming long-term girlfriends and getting married with the possibility of relocating overseas (Tsang, 2017a). In my analysis I suggest that reciprocating desire is an ongoing project of the self (Foucault, 1988) and that there is a connection with the state that requires sex workers to capitalize on their East Asian femininity.

For clients, desire involves finding someone with whom they have chemistry and can share intimacy. The sex worker–client exchange is subtle, yet powerful. In my conversations with high-tier sex workers, it was evident that in order to develop and attain success within their work, my respondents were expected to make efforts to cultivate a physical demeanour and social identity that would allow them to be recognized as "desirable" within their work space. The measures high-tier sex workers adopt to achieve desirability vary widely and depend upon the individual. For instance, some cultivate their professional identity by developing strategic interpersonal skills; some utilize effective marketing techniques to better engage wealthy clients; and some specialize in providing diverse and eclectic sexual and social experiences.

These high-tier workers highlighted body work and body capital that cultivates a desirable East Asian femininity. This femininity allows them to deal in recripocating desire with their clients. Both Rofel (2007) and Hoang (2014a) explore how upwardly mobile women navigate highly competitive urban environments to metaphorically and materially dress their bodies and sexual desirability to conform to how wealth and status are conceptualized within the context of East Asia. East Asian femininity operates as an "erotic oasis" (Delph, 1978), a specialized erotic world that caters to a plurality of desires, practices, and bodies.

As noted, the majority (34) of the sex workers come from well-to-do families. They had greater ability to be an "active agent" in determining which clients to pursue. For example, Dawning is a 23-year-old bar girl who comes from a cadre family in Shanghai. She believes that having tan skin might win sympathy from non-Chinese clients who will be loyal and return to buy her services. She noted that some non-Chinese clients think that tan skin symbolizes poverty (Hoang, 2014a; Stoler, 2002; McClintock, 1995). Dawning elaborated on this point by discussing her relationship with her long-term live-in boyfriend Mike. As a white male, Mike has an exaggerated sense of cultural superiority. He thinks of China as a Third World country and holds class- and race-based stereotypes about Dawning's dark skin and racial identity. McClintock (1995) noted that the whitening of black bodies is linked to the spread of Western civilization and the Victorian cult of domesticity with the new imperialism. Stoler (2002, p. 39) wrote that "control over sexuality and reproduction [was] the core of defining colonial privilege and its boundaries." The solution in a post-colonial era was white endogamy. The Western whites are the symbols of supremacy, and therefore tan skin symbolizes Third World dependency and can evoke sympathy from the Western white men. Mike says that he finds Dawning's petite and slender figure extremely feminine and cute. Dawning says,

> My small bones, waistline, hips, and breasts look more gentle, soft, and feminine. Probably these are the reasons why Mike became interested in me … I like tall, hairy, manly men. My live-in boyfriend Mike's blue eyes and blond hair look very sexy. Western men are more "polite" or better mannered than the Chinese guys.
>
> (Dawning, 23)

Some (16) sex workers were highly cognizant of the value male clients placed on submissiveness. These sex workers capitalized on body capital to signify different narratives and attributes associated with desirable femininity that are informed by racial and class politics. Coco, a high-tier sex worker from Guangdong, highlights how the intersections of race and gender frame how she approaches her work.

> Non-Chinese like Chinese girls who are docile and submissive. What I do is just listen to them and try to communicate with them. The non-Chinese

I meet want someone who is a caring and "normal" "wife." My magnetic and soft voice is enchanting and can "calm down the maniac and make men dance." I am an attentive listener; I have an appreciative laugh; and I give men affirmations that leave them feeling respected, admired, and masculine.

(Coco, 22)

Jan also comes from Guangdong and shares Coco's experience,

My clients find me coquettish and amorous [*fengqing wanzhog*風情萬種] and I have the most seductive eyes [*xiaohunyan*銷魂眼]. I just want to be provocative [*sao*騷] … I have a regular boyfriend who is an American. He likes my petite body and feels like he can protect me, which makes him feel like a real man!

(Jan, 25)

Pauline, a high-tier sex worker from Harbin, offers a commonplace insight that perfectly encapsulates the type of demands that such sex workers negotiate to maintain a highly constructed physical appearance. Specifically, the sex workers talk about the desires of their clients and how they subsequently adapt to expectations. Pauline notes:

Foreigners [*laowai*老外] like narrow eyes, dark skin, and a tall nose. So I will wear darker make-up since non-Chinese prefer tan skin. I had plastic surgery to heighten my nose so that I can look more charming and have a more bright and delicate silhouette.

(Pauline, 22)

Pauline's experience and the lengths she goes to in order to cultivate and maintain her physical appearance and sexual appeal are not atypical of sex workers who navigate Dongguan's high-tier sex industry. Amongst my respondents, various and multiple forms of cosmetic surgery (nose bridge alterations, double eyelid construction, and breast enlargements) were common.

Sixteen high-tier sex workers I met came from poor families. Despite their disadvantaged background, these sex workers capitalized on body capital to deal with desires. Zoe, a young and successful high-tier sex worker, had just finished her bachelor's degree and typified other sex workers who came from a disadvantaged background. She earns more than 60,000 yuan (US$9,677) per month. At 21, Zoe, who comes from a poor family in Sichuan, had the opportunity to travel to South Korea to receive various forms of facial cosmetic surgery on her eyes, nose, and chin because of her high salary. She said that, in addition to her extensive cosmetic surgery, her height (189 cm or around 6 feet) and self-described "good figure with a small waist and full breasts" have made her very popular "amongst big bosses and non-Chinese." Many respondents reiterated Zoe's sentiments and stressed the importance of maintaining a physical appearance described as feminine and attractive; it was typical for respondents to make strategic lifestyle choices to achieve their desired physical appearance. Tanning, restrictive diets, and regular trips to the gym were common.

The significance of how body work can be valued is also highlighted in the prevalence and significance of hymen reconstruction surgery, popular among sex workers in Dongguan. The surgery enables sex workers to simulate the breaking of the hymen during intercourse. Sex workers pursue this surgery because sex with a virgin commands a significantly higher charge than regular sexual encounters (Ding & Ho, 2013). Sex with a high-tier virgin sex worker can command up to 20,000 yuan (US$2,941). In my conversations with Gloria, a high-tier sex worker from a poor family in Guangdong, she admitted to getting hymen reconstruction surgery three times in the past three years.

> What men want is a virgin. I went for hymen reconstruction surgery at a female-centred plastic surgery clinic that my friend opened. Apparently, there are women lining up every weekend to get it done. You have to book an appointment too, or else you won't get in.
>
> (Gloria, 21)

Hazel comes from a poor family in Guangdong. She shares a similar experience:

> To be considered sexy by non-Chinese, one doesn't need to have a beautiful face, but definitely big breasts and a huge set of buttocks. I have had several nose jobs but the non-Chinese did not notice it so I tried to enlarge my breasts and include hymenography [i.e., surgical restoration of the hymen]. Of course, it works and they find I am more sexually appealing in bed.
>
> (Hazel, 21)

From the conversations of both the well-to-do and the disadvantaged sex workers, it can be concluded that there is not much contrast, despite their different class backgrounds. The emphasis that is placed upon recreating one's alleged sexual innocence – by providing the illusion of virginity – does not correspond specifically with socio-economic status.

Rather the emphasis that is placed on virginity is intimately tied to conceptualizations of desirable femininity, simultaneously sexualized and innocent.

Besides surgery and other types of physical alterations, many high-end sex workers discussed the type of aesthetic labour that they are expected to engage in (Warhurst & Nickson, 2009). Aesthetic labour refers to the effort needed to maintain a conventionally attractive physical appearance, which in turn affects one's marketability (Mears, 2014). Similar to body work, the aesthetic labour that sex workers engage in reflects the strategic steps that these women take in order to express cosmopolitan and desirable interpretations of femininity (Mears, 2014; Hoang, 2015). These female respondents were highly cognizant of the strategy and effort that were required of them to remain competitive within their industry. Many women discussed the transformative potential that their wardrobe and make-up offered them, particularly when they were expected to navigate expensive and elite social spaces. Moreover, by identifying and situating their aesthetic in relation to economic and cultural wealth and desirability, the high-tier sex workers interviewed said that they were able to achieve personal satisfaction. This satisfaction stems from cultivating a physical appearance that they recognize as conventionally attractive in addition to the professional success that comes from subscribing to an aesthetic presentation that is perceived as attractive and sexually desirable to their clients.

Reciprocating Desire from a Client Perspective

The value placed on presentation was also affirmed in the way male clients talked about femininity within the context of their experiences with high-end sex workers. In my conversations it was evident that male respondents did not have a singular conceptualization of idealized femininity. Their interpretations were informed by racial, sexual, and class-based interpretations of femaleness. During a conversation with Mike (Dawning's American partner), he implicitly offered insight into how class shaped his understanding of feminine desirability:

> Dawning has nice features like a feminine voice, sweet smile, expressive and submissive personality, and petite figure. She said it's because she grew up poor working on a farm. When she was young she didn't really take care of her skin. It wasn't until she went to the university that she started using skin care. It kind of hurt me a little bit as if I was looking at that little girl working hard in the field with a round-shaped Chinese

farmer hat during the hot summer day. I like her narrow eyes, long, silky-black hair, and slender body, feminine and colourful dresses with lots of lace. I just find her so arousing, sexy, cute, and sexually attractive.

(Mike, 39)

Derrick, who is Italian, has a highly racialized interpretation of his sexual preferences:

When I was young, I always fantasized about Chinese women who wear a Chinese gown and traditional Chinese dress like *qipao* [旗袍]. They are cute, cuddly, and adorable … very feminine indeed.

(Derrick, 32)

From Mike's description, Dawning's physical appearance does not comport with idealized Western femininity (Glenn, 2008). Rather, Mike discusses Dawning's femininity in relation to what he interprets as her comparatively lower socio-economic status. In effect, Dawning's body becomes a site wherein narratives of poverty and socio-economic struggle are played out so that Mike can attach romanticized, albeit highly classed-based, stereotypes to her demure presentation. Derrick, meanwhile, fancies Chinese women's petite figures; other non-Chinese clients shared similar views, noting that Chinese girls have a different temperament from women in their home countries. Sam, a Spaniard who has been working in China since 2007, defines what Asian femininity means to him:

Chinese women are more caring and have an expressive [情意綿綿] character. I don't know how to translate expressive [情意綿綿] … let me talk about May. May [who works in a high-end bar in Dongguan] is caring, cute, and charming. She wasn't a "whore" or a bar girl anymore, she never was, she was just a girl that happened to be on the wrong path. In front of my friends, she is polite and gives me lots of face. However, in our own world [bedroom], she gives me the most seductive and caring part of herself … Unlike Spanish women who are very direct, and demanding in bed. Like instructing me to fuck her aloud … she can fulfil my sexual hunger and thirst but can calm down my hot temper. She is pregnant and I will become a dad soon. According to my plans, I swear I don't want to have kids, but she changed my perception to form a family. She is very good at cooking and I love Chinese soup. Of course she prepares meals for me every day. At least my ex-wife did not treat me like this. I am living in a honey pot. I never felt like May was just doing it for the money.

(Sam, 36)

Many of the non-Chinese men agreed that long, silky-black hair, tan skin, and narrow eyes are the criteria for East Asian femininity. These non-Chinese did not express desire for a fair-skinned complexion, but femininity in reference to racial identity was prevalent. For instance, Victor, a 45-year-old white American man working in Dongguan, drew comparisons between Chinese and American women repeatedly to express his preference for "Asian femininity." In our conversations, Victor would often discuss his relationship with Pauline (22) by highlighting her physical appearance, using a highly racialized approach. Victor referred to Pauline's "silky-dark black-hair," her eye shape, and her petite-ness, which contrasted with his American ex-wife, whom he described as "fat." Women who engage with clients who have spent formative years outside of China and who have, previously, engaged predominantly with women outside of East Asia were highly aware of how their bodies become both a physical and symbolic tool. Their bodies enable them to express and communicate distinct forms of desirability that are fraught with the complexities of class, race, gender, and other factors. Jankowiak, Gray, and Hattman's Cross-Cultural Research study (2008) shows that 100 per cent of Chinese women selected Western male phenotype pictures as better looking than Chinese male photos.

Sex workers also are aware of how desires (and not merely sex) serve as important currency in attracting transnational capital. They make a determined effort to showcase their "partners"; they constantly give them "face" and support, which allows them to boost their clients' confidence. The trust-building process is important and can lead to direct investments in the Dragon Palace. Each of the 50 girls believed that their non-Chinese clients valued not only their beauty but also their ability to attract added business to these clients. As a bartender, I observed how bar girls would demurely pour beer, caress clients' arms or shoulders, and flirt. Through this type of attention, men feel "attractive" and "almighty" in the public sphere. According to Chen (2017), transnational working-class Taiwanese men who buy commercial sex in China signify a temporary upward mobility between social classes. The girls' well-off backgrounds play a crucial role in shaping their labour experiences and interaction with clients and their perception of self. In effect, sex workers recognize how their bodies become sites wherein narratives of wealth, poverty, race, and femininity intersect. As a result, sex workers can exploit narratives of femininity to instil feelings of desire, which in turn results in their own economic gain.

Sex Work and Individualized Desires

The significance and value placed upon body work and body capital was merely one component of how high-tier sex workers develop their professional identities. The manner in which these women accumulate such capital also provides them the framework to enact situationally appropriate forms of "desirability" (Lovell, 2000). The project means that they feel more individualized and can control the trajectory of their lives (Tsang et al., 2018). Within this line of work, those interviewed displayed a high level of awareness with regard to identifying the power and sense of identity that such capital afforded.

Materialistic Comfort and the Pursuit of Individualized Desires

As an example of how such capital is acquired, Zoe referred to the confidence she felt as a result of her strong command of the English language. Though this is somewhat of a prerequisite for those working in high-end bars, other workers nonetheless highlighted a range of wider credentials, be it forms of education or life experiences from their line of work. Vivian, a high-end worker from a middle-class background, spoke openly of the freedom afforded to her through sex work. In contrast to the low monthly salary she would have earned in medicine (US$806–$1,290), sex work provided a level of income that enabled her to work fewer hours while spending more of her time travelling:

> I graduated from a medical school and I earn about 50,000 yuan [US$7,246] every month excluding the money I have to give to my boss in high-end bar. I just work for about 10 days per month. It's quite relaxing and fun. Most of the time, I travel to places like Thailand, Italy, France, Australia, New Zealand, and other countries.
>
> (Vivian, 25)

Bonnie comes from Zhejiang and shares the same perspective about travel as Zoe and Vivian.

> I like travelling … my future plans involve living for a couple of years in America, then spending one or two years in Europe, then a couple more in Japan and so on, all over the world … That was what I had in mind when my boyfriend [in a dating relationship] took me to England … I don't really like China, and I imagine how good it will be if I could live in America, Britain, or Europe.
>
> (Bonnie, 22)

As is perhaps evident from such discussions, these sex workers fully embrace the cosmopolitan nature of post-socialist living in modern China. The pursuit of materialism and related processes serves as a key aspect of these workers' identities that enables them to construct a personalized lived experience within this environment (Chin, 2013).

Corruption and the Moral Vacuum in Post-Reform China

Phoebe (21) hated to inherit her parents' business, as she said that they are complicit with the cadres and professionals. Another woman, Elsa, said that she wanted to become a high-end sex worker because she did not want to be a cadre as arranged by her parents.

> I have been to Mexico, Colombia, and Latin America. My international character has emerged naturally since I have been dreaming of getting out of China. My father is a cadre and I know how corrupt he is. He has lots of mistresses and did not care for me but still gives me money. My English is excellent and I get used to travelling, making friends, and I think I will be able to adapt to a new culture easily. I wish I could find a foreign boyfriend to help get me out of China.
>
> (Elsa, 23)

In some ways, Elsa's parents served as an indirect reason for her falling into sex work, with the industry providing a form of financial gratification enabling possible relocation abroad and ensuring that she avoided the trappings of becoming a corrupted, morally questionable cadre (Link et al., 2013). Similarly, almost half of the 50 women interviewed admitted to perceiving a move overseas as a long-term desirable outcome. In this way the sex workers mirror the current state of post-socialist China: a collective of individuals such as the cadre-professional-entrepreneur paradigm focused on personal gain without consideration for wider societal improvements (Tsang, 2014).

The dynamic between cadres, professionals, and entrepreneurs remains a contested issue in modern China, often illustrative of Link's aforementioned "moral vacuum" (2013). Money has a functional meaning, but more importantly, it has the symbolic meaning of enabling one to be upwardly mobile and control one's life course, and therefore, to be "free" (Tsang et al., 2018). The most significant relationship within this network is that of the cadre, with both entrepreneurs and professionals conscious of the financial opportunities made possible via state-sponsored connections (Tsang, 2014). Conversely, a number of cadres have been known to utilize the same networks with multinationals as a means to line their own pockets. The crux of this issue is what Osburg

(2013) identifies as a form of highly controlled "elitist" masculinity: pluralized networks of corruption incorporating both cadres and much wider economic and professional networks.

Conclusion

I have adopted Hoang's and Rofel's conceptual framework to extend my thinking about reciprocating sexual desires using a comparative approach in a high-end bar. The concept itself expands upon these theories by examining how sex workers use their own body capital to create reciprocating desires and intimate relationships which in some respects mirror the wider desires of modern China, and specifically how the individual approaches China's post-socialist transition, structure, economy, and culture. As a result, sex workers – particularly those within the high-end market – recognize the need to cultivate idealized personas and physical identities for their own ends. High-tier sex workers perform labour in order to maintain an optimal physical appearance and cultivate a professional identity that complies with desires. Achieving this goal enables them to align themselves with dominant East Asian standards of beauty, which in turn facilitates upward economic mobility (Rivers-Moore, 2016; Hoang, 2015). In some ways, the performance of both workers and clients at times reflected a manifestation of engagement and manipulation of their own sexual expression as a tool for personal gain, with Dongguan's sex workers in particular – across both low- and high-end establishments – conscious of their bodies as conduits with which to improve their individualized desires and thus serve to better reflect post-socialist China as a consumer/individualized state. This chapter argues that both high-end and low-end sex workers capitalize economic reform and globalization in today's China to pursue their individualized desires. The Westernizing and individualized economy after the global financial crisis in China encourages a consumer revolution, which has come at the expense of being concerned with politics in Xi's regime and in turn is accelerating sex workers' focus on feeding their individualized desires.

Perhaps most importantly, the goal for creating reciprocating desire is the benefit accruing to the sex workers themselves. Providing the highest level of desire for the clients can change the dynamic of control for this elite sector of sex workers. Desire is a complex construct that has a link with genuine intimacy. When a sex worker can turn sexual desire into intimacy, the relationship can be transformed into one of mutual help and respect. Turning clients into partners is a logical goal, for the numerous reasons described here. Among this group of interviewees, it helps lessen the sting and stigma that their professional occupation is to give their bodies to strangers for money. Once intimacy is achieved, the sex worker can look in the mirror and see herself as a successful cosmopolitan woman of the world.

Despite the insights articulated here, there are two limitations in this chapter. First, the findings are limited to research respondents in Dongguan. Although Dongguan is a valuable field site, it is undeniable that China's commercial sex industry fluctuates from city to city. Secondly, the data presented in this chapter is exclusively from high-end sex workers. There is a vast literature on mid- and low-end sex workers detailing the pain and exploitation suffered by women involved in human trafficking. These women typically do not have the options afforded the high-end sex workers described here, and efforts to help and protect this population should continue. The data presented here simply acknowledges that there is a subset of sex workers who have been able to overcome the most difficult life conditions to gain a sense of personal value and self-worth.

Part 4 of this book is about social policy implications and criminal justice. Chapter 6 discusses selling sex as edgework in China's commercial sex industry. Chapter 7 examines criminal justice and the custody centre in China. After being arrested, female sex workers (mid-tier and low-end) and streetwalkers are sent to custody education centres (Re-education through Labour Camps, RTLC) throughout mainland China, where they are subject to societal stigmatization, violence and abuse, and varying forms of exploitation.

PART FOUR

Social Policy Implications and Criminal Justice

Chapter Six

Selling Commercial Sex as Edgework

I met Wendy at a mid-tier bar in Dongguan. She comes from Wuhan, Hubei. She was sporting a new outfit and showing off newly manicured nails. In our conversation, she revealed that she made enough money from sex work to quit. I asked: "Then why wouldn't you stop, if you have made enough money?" She stared at me blankly before answering,

> Five years ago, I told myself I would stay in this field for five years. Then five years went by and I am still in this field … It's not that simple … I feel like I am addicted to certain sexual activities. I get excited and thrilled. The sex thrill helps me forget my pain and reality … So now I feel that by [age] 30 I will become a businesswoman and open my own fashion shop … and I should be able to move on then … but who the hell knows? Fingers crossed [smiles].
>
> (Wendy, 24)

Wendy articulates an unremarkable, albeit emblematic, reflection on the complex position that she and her fellow sex workers face when considering the benefits, drawbacks, and possibilities that come with leaving the commercial sex industry. The notion of edgework is rarely applied to the sociology of female sex work in China, but it can help to explain why sex workers develop new skills, get married to Hong Kong businessmen, and decide to stay in the commercial sex industry. Edgework requires that sex workers recognize the risks in order to adequately navigate those risks. For some sex workers, risk can be effectively managed by employing risk reduction techniques that enable them to avoid on-the-job dangers. Moreover, for some, risk is not necessarily a negative aspect of the commercial sex industry. Rather, the risky aspects can give some sex workers positive feelings about their endeavours. It is acknowledged that for many sex workers, engaging in risky activities can present new opportunities to explore personal and sexual identity.

There are numerous risks inherent in these interactions, and only some can be controlled. Therefore, sex workers must weigh possible outcomes in terms of the resulting benefits or consequences. The notion of edgework as articulated by Lyng (2005) helps us understand the fine line between risky behaviour becoming pleasurable and manageable or turning dangerous and chaotic. By understanding how sex workers use edgework to remain in the commercial sex industry, we can understand the importance of these women's professional identities and social ties (Batchelor, 2007). By initiating a more complex approach to sex workers' experience with risk, this chapter fills a gap in the existing literature on China's commercial sex industry. It reframes the discussion on edgework as a conversation that includes the views and experiences of women.

This chapter is based on the 195 interviews conducted in the three niche markets. In addition, I also included 39 interviews from Hong Kong–based sex workers during summers in 2015–17. Many of these women reported that they returned to the mainland for a variety of reasons, but occasionally and regularly a number returned specifically to engage in sex work. Some respondents did this on a regular schedule while others worked sporadically. These respondents represent a niche segment of workers in the commercial sex industry. Their experiences are certainly not reflective of the majority of sex workers. However, this niche group is typically under-examined in existing scholarship. The dearth of literature on edgework suggests that there is a larger limitation in the wider discussion of the sex work industry and sex workers' unique experiences.

From Voluntary Risk-Taking to Edgework

When risk is tackled – in the context of academic literature – there is a concerted emphasis on exploring practices of risk management or risk reduction (Lyng, 1990; Lyng & Matthews, 2007; Short, 1984; Zinn, 2015). Within the realm of sex work, the literature on risk is well documented and heavily explored. However, on par with the discussion at large, the emphasis is generally on risk management and harm reduction. These risks can include health-related issues, including disease (Uretsky, 2016); insufficient economic autonomy (Tsang, 2017b); drug use and trafficking (Hoang, 2015); legal issues (Sanders, 2008b; Faugier & Sargent, 1997; McKeganey & Barnard, 1996); and physical harm or violence perpetrated by pimps, police, and customers (Zheng, 2009).

Stephen Lyng's nuanced discussion on edgework focuses heavily on voluntary participation in dangerous physical activities such as skydiving. He extrapolates that the attraction towards risky activities and the capacity to cultivate personal and psychological fitness and technical skills to effectively manage the anxieties and consequences effectively constitutes edgework. Such risk-takers engage in edgework to challenge themselves and master risks (Zinn, 2015, pp. 99–100). For action to be edgework, it must involve skill and control, not mere gambling or thrill seeking. Edgeworkers carefully cultivate their skills, and then take great pleasure in pushing these skills to their limits, towards "controlling the seemingly uncontrollable" (Lyng, 1990, p. 872).

For edgeworkers, risk has value and is its own reward. Risk offers edgeworkers a sense of meaning and agency. Individuals engaging in edgework may appear careless, but in fact they are rarely reckless. Instead, the edgeworker takes calculated steps to best control the outcome in highly risky situations (Zinn, 2015). Voluntary risk-takers are aware of the possibility of an adverse outcome. However, these judgments are based on experts' assessments, not on the risk-takers' assessments per se. Lyng's definition hints that, in order to maintain control, risk-takers are not always experts, nor are they fully cognizant of the danger in which they place themselves (Lyng, 2005; Tulloch & Lupton, 2003, pp. 10–11; Zinn, 2015, p. 100).

Originally, edgework was proposed as a synthesis of Mead and Marx to extend social action and alienation. As Lyng (2005, p. 9) notes, edgeworkers have the ability to control their emotions, value self-reliance, rebound quickly, and renew their own identity. Lyng described the common pattern of contemporary life: people feel alienated in a strange environment and survive by escaping the complicated social structure by embracing intense sensations of self-determination and control against the adverse circumstances (Miller, 1991). Although Lyng's discussion of edgework has been critiqued for being preoccupied with the experiences and subjectivities of young upper middle-class white men in industrial Western societies (Miller, 1991), his work provides a model that can help us understand why sex workers choose to stay in the commercial sex industry. Miller (1991) mentioned that risk is necessary for edgeworkers to see the thrilling activities as play. They will feel bored and lose interest if everything is too easy and under control. Edgeworkers believe that they can overcome the threat in a risky situation (Miller, 2005, p. 156).

Kong (2015a) has examined how male clients in Hong Kong are drawn to risky situations and practise risk management and personal forms of control in their interactions with sex work. However, his work focused solely on clients and not workers. Nicholls (2009) and Newmahr (2011) utilized edgework to understand women's experiences. Nicholls (2009) used edgework to explain how female street sex workers in the UK negotiate homelessness. Newmahr (2011, p. 160) used edgework to identify how men and women engage in physical, psychological, and, importantly, emotional risk-taking when engaging in sadomasochism. With this added perspective, women's experiences become more visible, making possible a new feminist perspective on edgework. That said, these works do not directly focus on risk in the commercial sex industry. This chapter bridges the gap between sex workers and edgework, articulating the complexities of risk within the context of how sex workers negotiate and find pleasure or satisfaction in the commercial sex industry.

Debates in the existing literature on the relationship between risk and gender have centred on women who were engaged in sexual edgework and women who were engaged in risk (Chan & Rigakos, 2002; Lois, 2005; Rajah, 2007; Stanko, 1997, p. 197; Walklate, 1997). Rajah (2007) mentioned that edgework may be differentiated across gender, class, and race. Edgework-resistance gives oppressed women the opportunity to experience the embodied rewards of self-authorship. Chan and Rigakos (2002) argued that women's experiences of risk are shaped by the politics of gender. Walklate (1991, p. 44) said that the gendered conceptualization of risk is a generated concept subjectively experienced. These existing literatures reinforce traditional masculinity, which values excitement, adventure, power, and control (Chan & Rigakos, 2002; Stanko, 1997; Tsang, 2018a; Walklate, 1997). Therefore, this chapter brings back the terms gender, class, race, and resistance-edgework (Rajah, 2007) to edgework studies. This is crucial to how risk is negotiated and understood. Female sex workers in China negotiate a multitude of dangers, and I argue that these risks are significantly more complex than the literature has acknowledged. Some risk is attractive, and while risk management is certainly an important aspect of sex workers' experience, it would be inaccurate to suggest that sex workers are always risk-averse.

Thrilling Sexual Desires and Creativity

Edgework is a voluntary exercise. Based on my samples, none of the women were overtly forced to become sex workers. More than 60 per cent said that they work for pleasure or for fun. Edgework relies on respondents enjoying the thrill of their jobs more than the fear of the consequences. For these women, it's all about experiencing exciting sexual desire and finding creative ways to thrill their clients. The respondents described selling commercial sex as a risk-taking and thrill-seeking activity. Some well-known activities brought added risk: bondage and discipline, dominance and submission, sadism and masochism (BDSM). Significantly, the girls also described risks in becoming emotionally involved with clients.

In sum, there are three major areas where edgework explains why some women choose to become – and remain – sex workers. First, the work focuses on thrilling sexual desires. Second, the work involves pleasure and reciprocal relationships with their clients and their co-workers; Third, the commercial sex industry rewards creativity and new skills or techniques in the workplace. Therefore, sex workers have an incentive to keep bringing excitement to their jobs. Simply put, clients will pay exorbitant sums of money to experience the most extreme, taboo physical acts.

Thrilling Sexual Desires

Many of the sex workers I talked with and interviewed in Dongguan admitted that, over time, they had become increasingly open and even partial to variations of BDSM. For many sex workers, participating in BDSM required learning new skills, but the burden was on them to practise them in a safe and manageable way. Through extensive experience, many sex workers learned to master the techniques and became comfortable in this area of their work. As a result, these sex workers found BDSM exchanges fun and worthwhile and often referred to them as an exciting part of their working experiences.

Xiaolin is a streetwalker from Hunan. Although streetwalkers are often the most exploited and downtrodden sex workers, Xiaolin is an exception. She is quite successful and enjoys the street life. She has a regular client who is a university professor. He often requests BDSM sessions where he wears long studded-leather boots. She says:

> I love being a docile "bottom." Bobby [the university professor] loves being dominant. Every time he comes, he brings along with him a leather bag with a dildo and an MP3 inside. I'd first need to turn on the music in the MP3 and dance to it in front of him, give him a strip tease. He masturbates as I dance. And when the dancing is finished, I use the dildo on him. One time, it took him more than an hour to come. I was so tired moving the dildo in and out, my hands were sore, so I accidentally hit his balls and he started crying. He also asks me to blow into his anus with a straw,

sometimes wants me to urinate as I give him a blow job, and he likes to fin-
ger me as he masturbates. I swear I'll never try these "strong appetite but
bizarre sexual activities" again. I couldn't really do it at the very beginning
because it was so weird. But I have to say, now, I cannot explain why, but
I like it. Perhaps I am stressed out about hiding the truth from my family
as a sex worker. These activities are exciting, hilarious, and wild. It allows
me to forget sorrow, pain, and boredom.

(Xiaolin, 23)

Another streetwalker, Huiling, shared the same experience as Xiaolin.
She says,

I can provide any service. Blow job, ass licking, "deep throating," you
know? Different clients like different services, some like blow jobs the
best, some like it when you lick their feet. I have all the sex toys, like dil-
dos, stockings, make-up, and costumes. I feel excited and I am so obsessed
with these activities. I enjoy being a sex worker as it is meant to be in my
life.

(Huiling, 23)

I originally met Linghan, a low-end sex worker, eight years earlier
when she was Qiqi and worked in a factory before entering the world
of sex work as Rabbit (discussed in the Introduction). As Linghan said,

Some people would bring girls they like to a private place for group sex
(nine sex workers and one client). There are lots of combinations, sometimes it could be four clients and six bar girls. Some clients want cosplay
like they become a queen and cross dress. I really like these activities
because it helps me to forget trouble, pain, and reality. I find these activities are very exciting and thrilling ...

(Linghan, 28)

Eight years earlier, as Qiqi (Rabbit), she had said:

I am open to many things, even if the client pees on my face, pees in my
mouth, and asks me to drink urine and taste shit [*huangjin shengshui*
黃金聖水]. One client required me to beat him and slap him. I remember
one day, I was tied to the ceiling with a red rope. I had candle wax all over
my shoulders, my breasts, my thighs, and marks on my ass from being
whipped. My hair had some of my client's semen on it too. At the very
beginning, I refused, no matter how much money was offered ... however,
I grew to accept it since I was so depressed and frustrated with lots of

things. I lost my parents within two months in 2016. After that, I become very accustomed and interested in these activities. Now I find these activities exciting and fun. I am actually addicted to my job ...

(Qiqi, 20)

Among all my 195 interviews, a significant number – more than 50 – of the sex workers emphatically and bluntly stated that they liked BDSM and providing niche sexual exchanges with their clients. But they also all admitted feeling bothered and sceptical when first introduced to these activities. That initial hesitation and uneasiness described by Linghan/Qiqi corresponds with testimonials of other types of edgeworkers. Lyng confirms that powerful feelings of anxiety, stress, and uncertainty are common for participants in high-risk sports. In effect, part of the process of dealing with risk is experiencing and managing the feelings of anxiety. People habituate and become desensitized to stimuli through repetition. In the same way, with experience, edgeworkers learn to overcome and master their fear.

In fact, sex workers said that, over time, these activities often became more thrilling and worthwhile than they had anticipated. There was an element of anticipation that heightened the experience they hoped to recreate. Specifically, these exchanges permitted the women to explore, then indulge themselves in, new aspects of their sexuality. This was an important component of their experiences. Moreover, the emphasis on personal discovery and exploring new forms of bodily pleasures corresponds with Lyng's finding on edgeworkers. Lyng highlights that, by participating in edgework, the individual is able to explore their identity and body with generative possibilities.

Pleasure and Reciprocal Relationship

Many women also said that their exchanges with clients allowed them to develop and explore new aspects of their personal identity. Sex work is more than just fulfilling a client's "special" needs. Many workers said they often enjoyed their work, and the reciprocal relationship with clients left them happy enough to stay in the commercial sex industry. The majority of those interviewed seemed to engage not only in hyperreality and the elongation of meaning (Ferrell et al., 2001) but also in mutual identification and a wide range of emotional and interpersonal services requiring unique skills. Hence, edgework is as much about finding the self as losing it, as much about escaping identity as reconfiguring it, and celebrating sex openly while in secret. In fact, positive and worthwhile interpersonal interactions with clients were cited as important elements of sex workers' overall experience. For many women, it was the social interactions that made their work interesting. Tiffany and Suling, mid-tier sex workers, and Dingding, a streetwalker, relay a sentiment that is shared by many others.

> One university student visited me twice per week. He did not know how to start and he was so shy and hesitant! I felt obliged to gently guide my virgin clients! Some clients who bump into me at the bar will buy me a drink, lunch, cakes, or a dessert. I find it so sweet and touching ...
>
> (Tiffany, 24)

> I can offer a place for my clients to seek psychological comfort. I am really willing to build friendships with my clients. Some will send me greeting messages and some even sent me mooncakes during Mid-Autumn Festival, which is touching. Because, I don't really treat them as "clients" but more as friends.
>
> (Dingding, 24)

> My relationships [with clients] are friendly. When they pass by my workplace, they will bring gifts and just visit, instead of asking for my services. A client who is a baker brought a freshly baked cake to me. Another client once gave me red packets [money] when his wife had a baby. I also hang out with my clients to have morning tea, hiking, travelling, and jogging. I think I am pretty much like a communal sweetheart.
>
> (Suling, 25)

Additionally, over 90 sex workers out of 195 highlighted the importance of the friendships forged with fellow sex workers, which were lost when they left the commercial sex industry. Shenman, a streetwalker from Chongqing, stressed the importance of those friendships.

> My sisters give me a shoulder to cry on if I feel depressed. I will call my sisters if clients refuse to pay or police give me trouble. We share common concerns, particularly those sisters who come from Chongqing. Emotional bonding is important for me.
>
> (Shenman, 34)

Even as interpersonal relationships, social networks, and the feelings of camaraderie with "sisters" are deemed important, relationships with clients are the proverbial "double-edged sword." Positive and worthwhile interpersonal interactions with clients were cited as important benefits to these sex workers' overall experience. Emotional labour involves interpersonal relationships. Sex workers are often best friends within the "sisterhood," but the professional distance from clients has to emphasize the sex-for-money transactional aspect and avoid developing intimacy.

Creative Endeavours to Learn New Skills

Most if not all of the sex workers interviewed noted that they had to develop certain performative skills and learn to maintain interpersonal boundaries. Performative skills are more than sex acts and positions. Performative skills are how the sex worker convinces the client that he is her best lover, friend, and even master. The goal is to make the client think that the worker cares about him so much that the cash exchange is just an afterthought.

The women interviewed displayed a certain element of pride that came with knowing they were experts at performance. Sexual skills are important in order for clients to believe that they are enjoying a genuine emotional connection (Tsang, 2017a). But it may be more important long term for sex workers to employ emotional labour and provide clients with emotional support. The girls listen to clients and engage them, helping them relax and feel at ease (Tsang, 2017a). Yet, ultimately, it was through these complex interpersonal exchanges with clients that sex workers were able to exercise unique skills and create experiences that made their work interesting. By developing ongoing relationships, sex workers treated their work as a creative endeavour. Feifei (mid-tier) and Jan (high-end) told me that they were always learning and enjoying performances with their clients, like acting, performing Chinese opera with full make-up and costumes.

> Some of my clients want me to wear a man's clothes; I will become a male prostitute for them. If they like the Monkey King [one of the Chinese opera characters], I grab my foundation and wig immediately. I can transform into 72 different Chinese creatures. Whatever they tell me to transform into, I will do it for them immediately. I have a performance desire and I love being on stage to perform. Being an actress was my dream when I was a child. I do it now for fun, fulfilling my childhood dream …
>
> (Feifei, 30)

> I love performing Chinese opera. I always have my hairnet, Chinese opera costumes, and manicured nails to sing Chinese opera. I feel really excited. I enjoy it for fun. I remember I can perform a "Shanghai baby" [Shanghai woman] series to my clients.
>
> (Jan, 25)

April (23) is a high-end sex worker. She told me that she loves dancing and some clients ask her to dance for them. She cannot resist showing off her pole-dancing, striptease, or belly dance. She also loves couples dances, such as the tango. Dancing with her clients makes her forget all her troubles. Some sex workers stay in the industry to learn new skills like cosplay, performing, and dancing. By learning new skills (mental fitness and technical approaches), the sex workers were able to expand the repertoire of exchanges, resulting in more variety, more pleasure, more pay, and therefore greater success.

In Lyng's deconstruction of edgework, he recalls Mead-Marx's insights on creativity and work. Specifically, Lyng draws on Marx's argument that, under capitalism, many jobs do not allow workers to engage in personal expression. Instead, labour often relies upon mechanized and repetitive action. Lyng revised his notion on risk, which focused more on actors' rational choice calculation and psychological motivations. His revised edgework framework followed that of Mead-Marx, which emphasized actors' risk-taking from a broader institutional social context (Lyng & Matthews, 2007, p. 78).

Unexpected Risks

Among the 195 sex workers interviewed, some told me that they sometimes underestimated the risks inherent in the commercial sex industry. They thought that they were experts, but they were uncertain about their risk-taking activities. The unexpected risks included the danger of sexually transmitted diseases (STDs), being caught by the police, and surprisingly, falling in love with clients.

Infection with STDs

Vivian, from a middle-class family in Harbin, had an experience that was not atypical for the high-tier sex workers with whom I spoke. Possessing a medical degree in China meant that she could only earn a monthly salary of between 5,000 and 8,000 yuan (US$806–$1,290), with long shifts and little time off. Therefore, she jumped to the sex industry to look for job flexibility and enjoy her life. She entered the sex industry for the money and excitement and described her job as a mix of customer service and fantasy fulfilment. She thought she was cautious and said she always used condoms. But one day she discovered she had contracted AIDS. With the help of local NGOs in Dong-guan, she is now tested each week for sexually transmitted diseases. She now insists on using condoms for all of her services: blow jobs, sexual intercourse, and cunnilingus. Still, the initial diagnosis was a shock for her.

> I felt like the world was collapsing in front of my eyes. I couldn't believe it. I didn't want to believe it ... However, I do not regret becoming a sex worker despite having AIDS. After I went to Los Angles to see AIDS experts, I feel better getting medication and treatment. My AIDS is under control. Life returns to normal and I can still work as a sex worker. I wasn't scared by AIDS enough to stop working as a sex worker.
>
> (Vivian, 25)

Vivian is a typical example of edgework. She told me that she does not want another job. She claims that only sex work gives her satisfaction and allows her to maintain her confidence and identity. Sex work gives her a reason to live and gives her life a sense of meaning. Vivian chooses to gamble rather than accept her condition and just wait for death. Most AIDS-positive patients in China believe that once they have AIDS they will not live for long. Vivian believes this too, but says that she wants a life different from "ordinary" women who work in sales or as secretaries. She feels that through sex work she can receive much more than she gives. She could quit her job, rely on her savings, and focus on improving her health. However, she believes that she can control and manage her unexpected risk by remaining in the sex industry. She says that, for her, new skills include learning how to give herself injections and control the growth of AIDS, and how to combat AIDS by adopting a more optimistic outlook on life. There were more than 20 sex workers who told me that they have different types of STDs. Like Vivian, they said that they overcame their psychological hurdles, learned how to cope with their difficulties, and stayed in the commercial sex industry.

Dealing with Police and Prison

Another unexpected risk faced by sex workers is regular police crackdowns, which force them to stay in custody centres after the Re-education through Labour Camp (RTLC) program.[1] Among the 195 respondents, a total of 55 female sex workers (10 from the mid-tier Lotus Club,

---

1 Custody education centres deploy many of the founding ideas that the RTLC program utilized to offer education that will allow sex workers to seek a better life after they leave the centre (Asia Catalyst 2013). More information can be found in the next chapter.

20 from the low-end bar Peach Bar, 25 streetwalkers) have either been detained in custody education centres or caught by police while engaging in sex work. I met Lotus, a low-end sex worker, in the summer of 2016 at her home after she was released from custody education for the second time. She told me her story.

She was caught with a client one day and forced to stay in the Dongguan custody centre, located in an isolated area out in the country. There she witnessed violence and exploitation throughout her stay. She says,

> I work 12 hours a day, seven days a week, each hour I have to sew 140 pairs of jeans, I only enjoy 1 day off per month. Do you know how much I make every day? I only make less than US$2 per day! I have to wear a bright yellow prisoner uniform, with the name badge put in front of my chest, and forced me to walk along the strip of downtown Dongguan. I was kept in one iron cage! The police even include my personal information like hometown and date of birth were printed in the badge too.
>
> (Lotus, 39)

The police intentionally forced Lotus to parade past others wearing bright yellow prisoner clothes, which is a shame and humiliation. Most of the sex workers were forced to work 12 hours each day with no breaks, performing tedious tasks like packing paper towels, disposable utensils, and Christmas products, and making paper flowers. After six months Lotus was finally released and she immediately returned to sex work. She said that, for her, it means freedom, money, and career prospects.

Kiki (34) is a streetwalker originally from Hunan. She has been arrested twice and also kept in the custody centre for six months. During her first arrest, the police barged into her room unannounced while she was servicing a client. The police forced her to strip and pose for a picture with her client, then demanded she confess to being a sex worker. When Kiki refused, she was subsequently beaten up by the police. They hit her head, body, and feet, and grabbed her hair until her skin and eyes were swollen, purple, and red.

Nevertheless, Kiki refused to confess. Eventually, the police gave up or grew tired and asked her to leave. She did not pay any fine that night. The second encounter happened after a dissatisfied client reported her to the police. The police swooped in, arrested her, and took her to the police station. There she was taken into a room and beaten by a group of police until she could not tolerate the pain. She confessed that she was a prostitute; under Chinese law, she could now be sent to the custody centre in Dongguan for six months. When Kiki was released, she too immediately went back to sex work. Kiki said one reason was to make up for the fines and debts from her sentence, but she also emphasized that she loves her work.

It is estimated that over 400,000 beggars and juvenile criminals were detained in 310 custody centres in 2007 all over China (Wu, 2007). Sex workers are subject to administrative penalties including official warnings, fines, writing self-criticisms, short-term detention, or longer-term incarceration. An estimated 500 sex workers are killed every year in China (Hunter, 2005). Lotus, Kiki, and other detained sex workers say they are now more vigilant and able to avoid arrest. They do not want to go back to the custody centre. When released, the 55 sex workers immediately returned to their jobs. As edgeworkers, they can cope with the risks.

Emotional Risks with Clients

Sex work is more than just fulfilling client's "special" needs. Most of the women interviewed said that they enjoyed their reciprocal relationships with clients. Edgeworkers in this industry can control their emotions as they build relationships with clients, but they need to refrain from falling love with them. Most sex workers have already set up their bounded authenticity (Bernstein, 2007) with their clients. Olivia and Kitty, both low-end sex workers, relay a common sentiment:

> I have a very good body and gigantic breasts. I can have orgasm three or four times per day ... I think it was meant to be for me to become a sex worker. However, a guy who is only aged 35 is obsessed with me. And I am 42! Whenever we go out, he holds my hands. He sleeps in my house probably three or four nights a week. But I know probably he needs my money and I have to be detached from him ... Falling in love with a client who is younger than me and I have to feed him [*baoyang* 包養] is a disgusting and stupid thing ...
>
> (Olivia, 42)

> I have fallen in love with one client before. Later, I found out he had a record of domestic violence. One day he beat me half to death. It caused bone damage and I could barely walk. He believed that I could not be a sex worker again if I was crippled. I was unable to even turn around; hence, I could not work and even could not take care of myself. It took me two months to recover. After this experience, I needed to back off and set boundaries with clients although they chase after me ...
>
> (Kitty, 48)

That said, the sex workers encounter romantic risk and they have to set up bounded authenticity to deal with desires, intimacy, and romance with clients. Most sex workers recognize that they need to clearly separate their professional and personal lives. They have to differentiate between providing emotional labour and maintaining professional distance.

Alienation, Discrimination, and Identity Crisis

The second set of data examined sex workers who migrated to Hong Kong from mainland China by way of marriage. This fits perfectly with Mead-Marx's framework on edgework, which emphasized actors' risk-taking within their own environment and linked it up to a broader institutional social context. The 39 interviewees had worked and resided across urban Guangdong prior to moving to Hong Kong. However, before living in the Pearl River Delta Region, the majority of the respondents originally came from rural communities across China. For many of these women, Hong Kong was an important part of their upward economic mobility and social status. Hong Kong's cosmopolitan status was significantly higher than that of second-tier cities such as Dongguan and Huizhou. However, despite being an "upward" transition, the move to Hong Kong often resulted in emotional, interpersonal, and cultural alienation. In Hong Kong the women did not have significant or familiar social networks, and eventually their loneliness turned to boredom, which led to bouts of depression. Among my respondents, all 39 agreed that they had no financial problem living in Hong Kong. Over 20 of them expressed their willingness to occasionally come back to the commercial sex industry. The problem was the loneliness and alienation that made them long for the familiar, exciting risks associated with their old career.

The experience related by Yifan is typical. Yifan is a 23-year-old from Kunming who previously worked at the high-tier Dragon Palace. She earned a lot of money and saved enough to leave the industry entirely. She moved to Hong Kong and now says that she misses her life in China. She cited multiple reasons why she felt alienated after moving to Hong Kong, which is why less than a year later she regularly returns to China for commercial sex work. It's not about money; Yifan has a monthly stipend of 28,000 yuan (US$3,856) provided by her husband. He gives her this in lieu of what she would have earned had she stayed in the commercial sex industry. Yifan says,

Every time I go to a karaoke lounge, I can't help but show off my pole-dancing skills. I haven't adjusted to the Hong Kong lifestyle and society yet ... I'm so far away from my "sisters," it's very boring and I can't speak Cantonese ... So sometimes I talk to the sisters and find a part time gig or two [as a sex worker, back in China] just to kill my boredom.

(Yifan, 23)

For other women who have seemingly "married up," sex work continues to be a fixture in their lives to varying degrees. Tina shares a similar experience with Yifan.

After two years of staying in Hong Kong, I have re-entered the sex industry [back in China]. When "my sister" has her period, I will replace her and stay in Dongguan for two or three days. But, I always relapse ... and that's what it feels like: a relapse. Of course, I won't let my husband know and I only do it when he has a business trip ... I shouldn't do that, but only in sex work can I find my lost identity and I feel thrilled.

(Tina, 32)

Tina revealed to me that she has more confidence as a sex worker. The lost identity reflects Tina's self-image. Women such as Yifan and Tina represent sex workers who have financial and personal security, which renders sex work more a hobby than something done out of need. They are motivated by familiarity with the commercial sex industry and the excitement of being with the particular circles of sex workers (and clients) with whom they worked. Their stories reveal that financial and personal security do not necessarily ensure that some women will permanently leave the commercial sex industry. Although most interviewees did not have the high levels of economic security enjoyed by Yifan and Tina, many said that the important thing was to maintain their own economic independence.

Luping also said that relationship problems coupled with the desire to be financially independent eventually led her back to the commercial sex industry. After she married her Australian husband, David, she soon realized that they simply didn't have much in common. She couldn't go back to the bar and work, so she started finding part-time work and taking English lessons. She says,

David also spent US$1,000 per month to hire an Australian teacher to teach me English and computer skills. Then I realized that this is not something I could do. I could not even work as a receptionist or in sales! I felt a little sad when I realized all I really knew was how to be a sex worker. I sleep until noon then get up to cook. One day, I told my husband "Maybe I should go back to the bar … I don't want to suffer like this, even though I might need to sleep with some gross men, I wouldn't be this tired." After our honeymoon period, a lot of problems started to come up between us. For example, we didn't like the same films and we didn't share the same hobbies or lifestyle. Our love is fading and our relationship is on the brink of collapse …

(Luping, 29)

Yifan, Tina, and Luping revealed that their "economic security" depended upon their marital status, and they put it at risk by engaging in sex work. This form of "edgework-resistance" (Rajah, 2007) vividly reflects how these women are tempted to return to the commercial sex industries, but at the same time, they fear losing their economic security and their husbands. Social and professional networks are crucial. Many sex workers affirmed that their social networks are vital in shaping their feelings about the commercial sex industry. Moreover, when they were faced with losing access to social networks and important friendships, certain personal struggles were exacerbated. For instance, the loss of personal social networks was made worse by the women's inability to speak Cantonese in Hong Kong, which resulted in further discrimination (Lowe & Tsang, 2017). A comment by Lok highlights how the cultural alienation and the (Putonghua-Cantonese) language barrier resulted in greater personal dissatisfaction and affected her mental health

Discrimination is very serious because I don't speak Cantonese. I can only speak Putonghua. Therefore, I cannot make friends and my social life is horrible … I need friends who I can talk with; otherwise, I cannot survive …

(Lok, 26)

Yaoji offers a similar insight:

When I speak Putonghua, Hong Kong people stare at me and get annoyed. They yell at me and their voices are very loud, I find it annoying and disgusting … The cultural and social conflict between Hong Kong and China is getting very serious … I feel like I cannot find friends in Hong Kong. Therefore, I start contacting my "sisters" who are working in China. It is easy for me to talk to them and they really understand me.

(Yaoji, 26)

Some of the reasons why former sex workers will return to the commercial sex industry after migrating to Hong Kong have been identified. By understanding the motivations and circumstances that lead women back into the commercial sex industry, we can identify the risks that respondents face in migrating to Hong Kong. Their reasons for returning vary in severity: bouts of depression; varying forms of discrimination and isolation; and loss of personal autonomy. Taking these circumstances into account, it appears that respondents negotiate risks outside of sex work that lead them back into sex work.

Clearly there are risks that come with participating in the commercial sex industry. The women migrating to Hong Kong were faced with unique opportunities as well as unanticipated challenges in their personal lives. Many were left unsatisfied because of the discrimination and alienation they experienced as mainlanders. These women encountered a range of obstacles that were uniquely difficult to deal with. The social, cultural, and personal alienation that they felt was significant and created feelings of dissatisfaction and isolation. Although many women cited negative experiences as sex workers, many of the respondents did not find that migration to Hong Kong, alone, improved their circumstances, given that migration had subsequently created new anxieties and conflicts that they struggled to negotiate. Derogatory slurs such as "Shina," "dai luk lo" (大陸佬), "dai luk por" (大陸婆), or even the degenerate "Ah Chaan" (阿燦 literally, "the uneducated" or "the hayseed") are used to describe mainlanders. Additionally, disidentification with Putonghua by associating it with the atavistic or feminine affirms Cantonese as the masculine (Lowe & Tsang, 2017). While many Hong Kong people and mainlanders share similar phenotypical markers of identity and primordial origins as descendants of the Han Chinese, many Hong Kongers continue to identify themselves in opposition to mainlanders and remain unapologetic in their exclusionary attitudes. In effect, the distinction between mainlanders and Hong Kongers as separate Chinese groups is built on the basis of geo-historical, sociopolitical, and cultural differences cultivated during the British colonial presence in Hong Kong.

The sex workers who married Hong Kong businessmen have the ability to develop intense feelings of self-determination and control to counter adverse circumstances. The sex workers feel alienated in Hong Kong because of sociocultural differences like the language barrier and lost identity. At least some of the respondents failed to adjust to their new life in Hong Kong. Lacking the necessary social support, they found the hurdles of migration uniquely challenging, and this pushed them to reconsider sex work as a way to regain their lost identity. Hiding that truth from their husbands was a risk they could at least control. All in all, sex work seemed to offer something familiar and desirable, in contrast to a new environment full of obstacles and personal conflicts.

Conclusion

The insight and reflection on the experiences of a niche community of sex workers help us better understand their motivations to stay in the commercial sex industry and even return after having left it. The experiences described here have been placed within the context of edgework and help us extend the literature and expand the dialogue on the commercial sex industry in China. Existing discourse on risk and sex work has suggested that sex workers are unanimously averse to experiencing any types of risk. But by utilizing edgework, it can be argued that these women may be attracted by the very risk this activity presents. The concept of edgework attempts to reframe the stigma and negativity that shape dominant understandings of risk. The chapter provides a new and necessary lens to understand the diversity of sex workers' experiences and motivations.

Specifically, this chapter draws upon two sets of data to apply Lyng's concept of edgework. One set of data was taken from in-depth interviews with sex workers from different niche markets in Dongguan. The edgework concept has offered insights into how sex workers take interest in and derive pleasure from engaging in risky activities that produce thrilling sexual desires and encourage distinctive types of creativity. These pleasures and satisfactions include exploring bodily pleasure and new aspects of sexuality; work in a relatively unstructured environment wherein they can work dynamically and creatively to realize financial gain as well as adulation and emotional reward. Another significant aspect of these accounts is that the sex workers need to deal with unexpected risks to avoid physical dangers (STDs) and personal entanglements (emotional risk ties with clients).

Finally, based on the accounts of 39 former sex workers who married Hong Kong businessmen, this chapter has explored the struggles of leaving the old life and trying to start a new one in Hong Kong. Through the lens of edgework, these women might be expected to use their dynamic energy and resourcefulness to adapt and easily make the transition. However, it is interesting and not too surprising to find that struggles with alienation and isolation in Hong Kong resulted in a number of women admitting that they longed for their old life. The thrill of illicit sexual pleasure may be a permanent part of their self-identity, a part that is too tempting for these "tempting girls" to resist. To go back to sex work, even if on a temporary or occasional basis, helps these edgeworkers reclaim their professional life and glory in the thing they do better than anyone else.

The next chapter discusses criminal justice and custody education. It argues that custody education is a form of governmentality and treats the detained sex workers as examples of the *homo sacer* in order to maintain stability and harmony. The concept of biopolitics and *homo sacer* will be used to argue that custody education is rarely a source of rehabilitation; instead it is a strategic moneymaking enterprise that helps facilitate corruption within local law enforcement and propagates anti-sex worker sentiment.

Chapter Seven

Profit-Making Disguised as Rehabilitation: The Biopolitics of the *Homo Sacer* in China's Custody Education Program for Sex Workers

I met Lotus privately at the Peach Bar, the bar where I conducted the bulk of my research on the low-tier sex industry in Dongguan. As I followed Lotus into a private room, I admired her ability to walk gracefully in her five-inch platform heels. A man loitering in the hallway took an interest in seeing two women enter the same room together, but otherwise just stood and watched. The room was dark and reeked of mouldy cigarettes, mildew, and laundry detergent.

Lotus motioned me to a chair and I sat down. She slowly paced around the room and began to share her story. Through teary eyes, Lotus told me that the money she made from sex work allowed her to support her 16-year-old daughter. I was not sure how to react. Should I stand up and give her a supportive hug, or would that be crossing a line? Instead, I sat quietly and listened. She pulled up a chair and sat down next to me. In an even voice she said, "Is it really difficult to become a sex worker? It's not like someone made the choice for me. But I think if I had other options I would not be doing this." I tried to console her by lightly patting her shoulder, and she flashed a tight smile at me. After a brief silence, she remarked: "I am going to tell you what I experienced in the custody centre." As she began to confide in me and show her trust, I cemented the deal by motioning for a drag of her cigarette. As we shared the smoke, Lotus confided her experience of being detained.

The centre is at an undisclosed and isolated location somewhere in Dongguan. The facility operates as a cross between a prison and a factory, where the residents face an exhausting work schedule and substandard living conditions. Over the course of her six-month-long detention, Lotus worked 12 hours per day, seven days a week with no breaks. She was given tedious tasks to complete for a nearby factory. In desperation, she said, she had to seek help in creative ways:

> I once slipped a written note into a jeans pocket. I hoped the foreigner who might buy the jeans would report this inhumane treatment to the mass media. I know most of the jeans I was making were shipped to the USA or Europe. I cannot say one word here in China. People would think I am an idiot, and they won't believe I am an inmate. The note said [in Chinese]: "Dear customer, if you buy these jeans and see this note, please help me and spread this message to the world: I am a sex worker and am now being held in a custody centre to do sewing work ... I am paid less than US$2 per day! However, our boss – the Chief of Police – receives lucrative profits from the factory boss. China is the only country in the world running custody centres as such a lucrative business. It is not only for myself, but for the thousands of people kept in custody education centres in China who are under the persecution of the Chinese Communist Party Government. I thank you for your help" ...
>
> (Lotus, 39)

Over the course of my research, numerous female sex workers – primarily streetwalkers and workers from the low- and mid-tier commercial sex industry – provided strikingly similar accounts. They described the exploitation and sometimes violence they experienced in being charged by police for solicitation and sale of sex work, then subsequently detained in custody centres.

Custody education centres deploy many of the founding ideas that Re-education through Labour Camps (RTLC) utilized. The centres, unlike the prison system, were conceived and designed to prioritize the rehabilitation process (Smith, 2012) and target "criminals" who have committed non-violent crimes. These "criminals" have typically been compromised because of their economic, health, and social positions. This category of criminals includes sex workers, beggars, and drug users. Unlike prisons, custody education is intended to offer an environment wherein detainees can develop practical life skills and access services and education that will allow them to seek a better life after they leave (Smith, 2012; Asia Catalyst, 2013).

Since 1949, the Chinese Communist Party has made a concerted effort to control and minimize the commercial sex industry by criminalizing all aspects of sex work: solicitation, sale, and purchase (Human Rights Watch, 2013). Since sex work is typically categorized as an administrative offence, it is entirely possible to be charged for the solicitation and sale of sex work and not go through typical litigation channels (Human Rights Watch, 2013; Asia Catalyst, 2013). Instead, detainees are processed through locally run administrative detention systems. Notably, individuals suspected of administrative offences may receive fewer forms of protection than offenders in the typical criminal system. Offenders charged in the criminal system technically have access to a lawyer and are tried and sentenced by a court composed of a three-judge bench. That said, similar to custody education, the procedural rights of prisoners are also routinely violated and ignored by the judicial system. In addition to the lack of protection that detainees in custody centres receive in terms of their options regarding legal proceedings, they also must negotiate a detention culture riddled with abuse and exploitation between staff and offenders. The decentralization of Custody Education means that there is minimal oversight of detention centres. This has resulted in detainees being given inappropriate forms of punishment and inadequate protection. Furthermore, these circumstances and lack of oversight have made detention centres a space to facilitate corruption.

In the niche body of literature that tackles the commercial sex industry, there is insufficient attention devoted to the abusive practices directed towards sex workers detained in custody education centres in Asia or in China. There is limited literature published in English that mentions the operational mismanagement of these custody centres; the exploitative deals made between law enforcement and commercial factories; and the daily and systematic violence directed towards vulnerable offenders. The dearth of literature on sex workers' experiences in custody education centres is hardly surprising. It's not that scholars or public health professionals lack interest in this subject, but access to custody centres and the mainland criminal justice system is so limited that they become, for all practical purposes, invisible.

In order to understand the ideological and political impact of custody education centres and their effect on the lived experience of sex workers and their identities in the public sphere, the notion of *homo sacer* serves as a generative conceptual tool. The figure of the *homo sacer* as a human being stripped of basic human rights, articulated by Giorgio Agamben in his discussion of refugee camps, provides an intriguing explanation of why sex workers are excluded from public discourse. Agamben wrestles with the impact of this exclusion and how such exclusion articulates a moralistic notion of acceptability and a particular societal imaginary. The full complexity of the *homo sacer* suggests that violence against those so designated is entirely permissible. The *homo sacer* is a figure that has been stripped of political status and has no legitimate standing. These centres ultimately prioritize the financial and personal needs of local law enforcement. The detention culture that has been created seems content to marginalize sex workers both during and after their sentences.

It is difficult to understand the plight of female sex workers detained in custody education centres because there is so little published data on these experiences. Ethnographic data provided by female sex workers who have been detained will shed light on the experience surrounding detention and rehabilitation. Interviews with these women recognize their lived experiences inside custody education centres, and their testimonials offer evidence of police abuse. To develop a comprehensive understanding of sex workers' experiences, such accounts are vital. Moreover, the day-to-day realities of custody education stand in contrast to the underlying ideologies and aims behind the system and the guiding principles of re-education.

Agamben's *Homo Sacer*

The plight of sex workers in China aptly reflects Giorgio Agamben's conceptual framework of biopolitics and *homo sacer*. Published against the backdrop of exposing the totalitarianism that is hidden deep inside Western democratic societies,[1] Agamben (1998) begins his genealogy by differentiating *zoe* and *bios*. *Zoe* refers to the simple living conditions common to all, while *bios* refers to the appropriate form of living for individuals or groups. *Bios* connotes life with particular rights and dignities of citizenship (Spencer, 2009; Ziarek, 2008). *Homo sacer* is a term describing those individuals who exist outside of *bios* and only occupy *zoe*. In that space, the *homo sacer* is stripped of rights and maintains an extra-legal relationship with the law by being excluded from it (Agamben, 1998, pp. 181–8; DeCaroli, 2007). Within the colonial societies of India and Pakistan, Jabbar explained the empirical exertion of control over the bodies of sex workers and their subaltern resistance through the modalities of religion and imperialism (Jabbar, 2011, 2012).

---

1 Modern democratic states, Agamben argues, have the ability and right to deprive citizens and human beings of their rights. In places of exclusion such as refugee camps, inmates are merely allowed to have rights of which they can be deprived, as they lack the right to have rights.

The Application of the Homo Sacer *to Female Sex Workers*

Foucault (1982/1988, p. 146) argued that "sex was a means of access both to the life of the body and the life of the species." Therefore, it is necessary to look at the regulation of sex and the body of the sex worker to understand the role that sex plays in the analytic of power in post-reform China. More importantly, Agamben's notion of the *homo sacer* shows the extent to which sexuality and sex work are repressed by the government.

From the East Asian perspective of mainland China, Agamben's theory provides a grounded conceptual understanding of the empirical phenomena of rural-migrant sex workers in China's reform camps. The Chinese reform camps are places that constitutively include migrant sex workers by virtue of their exclusion from the legal order. From a biopolitical standpoint, these rural migrants lack the legal rights of abode in urban cities without *hukou*, effectively excluding them from *bios*. Instead they are subject to the totalitarian political control over their bare life in such reform camps (*zoe*).

The result is the process by which democracies are transformed into totalitarian regimes. It begins with good intentions but breaks down into a bad practice, similar to the state-sanctioned policies allowing the detention of terror suspects without trial. So also the social forms of asylum-seeking designated as "newly transnational," from a historical perspective at least, are a useful corrective to the kinds of political universality that European nation states have been in the habit of espousing since the the classical age.

The near-absolute knowledge system that makes up the dominant culture encourages us to believe in this liberal-utopian myth. For every Eurocentric form of knowledge about "other peoples' way of life," the cases of rural-migrant sex workers held in reform camps represent modes of resistance against the prevailing order. Those cases are pockets of subversion that challenge our normative paradigm, and instances of subaltern "minority" existence that challenge the dominant discourse. By stripping rural-migrant workers of their right to live in urban spaces because of their involvement in prostitution, the biopolitical treatment of these workers creates the figure of the *homo sacer*. Their sexual deeds are thus deemed immoral enough to render them "sacred," as they have been tainted by the vices of prostitution – an illegal act in modern China that carries severe penalties of imprisonment. In reform camps, rural-migrant sex workers are included in the nation's criminal justice system by their exclusion from the fabric of urban China's societal system. In the social sciences, there is a shift towards understanding the "embodied" nature of prostitution as a social practice. Scholars of sex work have attempted to explain how the regime detaches the human body of the female sex worker as an objectified, discrete entity or element from its symbolic value in native post-reform Chinese society.

Custody Education and Its Historical Context

Since 1949, the laws on sex work and the structure of detention facilities have changed at various points. It was only in the 1980s that the custody education centres became a designated facility for offenders charged with sex-work offences (Asia Catalyst, 2013). Additionally, not only has the imposition of anti-prostitution laws in 1991 and 2006 continued to criminalize sex work, but these laws have also made sex work increasingly dangerous, particularly with regard to laws that pinpoint condom possession as evidence of sex work.

Custody education employs punishment guidelines for offenders charged with offences related to sex work. If the offence is deemed "minor," the detention may be one week or a fine of 500 yuan or less (Human Rights Watch, 2013). For typical "normal" offences, detentions can last anywhere from 10 to 15 days and include fines up to 5,000 yuan (Human Rights Watch, 2013). Repeat offenders under the Re-education through Labour Camps (RTLC) program may have to serve a sentence from six months to two years; otherwise, offenders with a limited record may serve their detention under an "educational administrative measure," which can also last between six months and two years (Human Rights Watch, 2013). The normal maximum sentence in a custody education centre is two years, although in rare cases an offender may be detained longer than this period. Despite the lack of detailed information, experts estimate that anywhere from 18,000 to 28,000 women are sent to detention centres each year. The number of centres grew to 200 by 2005 (Zhang, 2014).

As mentioned earlier, the relative silence surrounding custody education is part of the greater silence in China on issues relating to the criminal justice system. An example of the minimization of and disengagement from such dialogue is found in the central government's treatment of figures such as Harry Wu (Hongda) (1937–2016). Wu, a Chinese dissident who migrated to the United States after enduring 19 years as a political prisoner, has shed light on the re-education labour system. As a university student, Wu was imprisoned in 1960 for openly criticizing the 1956 invasion of Hungary by the Soviet Union. After nineteen years of imprisonment in a labour reform camp (*laogaidui* 劳改 队), Wu was released in 1979. In his book (Wu, 1992), he offered a bitter and emotional account of the cruelty and unfairness of "re-education" through forced labour. Wu asserts that it is specifically "designed to physically and spiritually destroy human beings" (Wu & Vecsey, 1996). Wu's work is part of an integral, albeit minor, body of literature that prioritizes the lived experiences of former prisoners in order to deconstruct the *laogai* (劳改) system, which has been deceptively packaged as a seemingly innocuous rehabilitation program (Wu, 1992). Despite receiving human rights awards and being hailed as a hero in the West, Wu has been denounced in China as a traitor and spy (Spence, 1996).

Charging Prostitutes

The manner in which sex workers are typically charged for their crimes is distinctly unjust. Zhuohua, a streetwalker who comes from Anhui, had a similar harrowing tale to Kiki's, described in the previous chapter:

> I was surprised. I would have never believed someone could treat me with so little humanity. Don't I have any rights? The police woke me up by throwing cold water on me ... I was beaten up and vomited a lot and was being forced to eat my own vomit. I was beaten until I lost consciousness ... I guess at that time, the police needed to fill a quota or maybe they needed money or they were just in a bad mood ... or some soon-to-be retired police needed more money for their retirement ... I don't know. They tied me to a tree and threw boiling water to torture me. Of course, they also humiliated me by using lots of foul language and forced me to confess I am a whore. I refused to confess regardless how hard they bullied me. However, they did not let me go and finally I was detained for three months.
>
> (Zhuohua, 36)

Living Conditions in the Custody Centre

Unlike the prison system, custody education claims to incorporate a rehabilitative approach that seeks to reorient the detainee's moral compass and their ideological positioning to better situate them with the ideological, political, and economic demands of the state. In line with such aims, physical labour has traditionally been a component of most detention sentences. However, physical labour is ideally only intended to be a minor portion of a detainee's sentence (Miller, 1982; Smith, 2012), alongside a rigorous diet of moralistic and ideological pedagogy. This comes in the form of structured reading activities, counselling sessions, meetings with social workers, and other activities. On the one hand, these activities are designed to provide detainees with practical skills that will help them when they leave the centre and return to civil society. However, in reality, sex worker detainees rarely participate in any organized retraining and self-betterment activities. Instead, according to the respondents, they spend the majority of their time in highly strenuous labour. This stands in contrast with the supposed designated purpose of custody education, which is to provide detainees with the necessary skills and tools to leave the life of crime that originally brought them there.

However, the women I interviewed returned to sex work after leaving the custody education centre. They all gave a variety of reasons, but the most prevalent was to gain economic stability and to repay debts that they incurred during their sentences. Xiumen, a low-end sex worker, notes,

> I had to pay for my living expenses in the centre including sexually transmitted disease tests and therapy costs. But these costs are always much higher than regular hospitals and clinics. I was forced to have a STD examination but they didn't tell me the results of the test ... I also paid about 300 yuan [US$48] in living expenses per month.
>
> (Xiumen, 36)

Xiaohua is a mid-tier sex worker from Dongbei and works in the Lotus Bar. She echoes Kiki's claims:

> The Chinese government, police, capitalists are bribing each other and running custody education as a business and making a lucrative profit ... I was in there for six months and, of course, I had to pay my daily expenses. The toiletries are very expensive, at least triple the price of buying from the supermarket. Only rich people can be in jail, and poor people like me cannot survive. I've spent 10,000 yuan [US$1,612] in six months. When I was released, I immediately went back to be a sex worker since I had to pay fines and debts from my sentence. This is very ironic because I'm not supposed to go back to it after being "rehabilitated."
>
> (Xiaohua, 29)

Meihua, a low-end sex worker originally from Guangdong, describes similar circumstances that ultimately lead her back to sex work.

> ... If I am sick and need medicine it will be deducted from my salary. I don't think there is a need for a custody education, the purpose of "re-

education rehabilitation" is twisted. I was just working for the police, I didn't have a salary. When I left the centre in February [2016], I immediately returned to being a sex worker. The custody "education" did not change my mind or encourage me to change my career. I earn more than 8,000 yuan [US$1,290] a month which is three times more than working-class workers with no skills. Why do I have to give up my job?

(Meihua, 39)

Meixia comes from Guangdong and works in a low-end bar. She says,

I've used all my savings during my time in the custody centre. I still have my son in my hometown and my mother takes care of him. When I was so broke, I could not afford to pay for my daily expenses in the centre. The police asked me to give them a name to contact. They called my mother. Of course, my mother did not ask any questions. But she is so quiet now, and I know she is ashamed ...

(Meixia, 37)

Yuemiao, a streetwalker from Jilin, describes the high costs that come with living in custody education centres.

I paid 1,700 yuan [US$274] which included 200 yuan [US$32] monthly living expenses and another 500 yuan [US$80] extra for bedding, a uniform, and daily products like toothpaste ... I was required to purchase all of my daily products. The stores inside the centre charged at least triple that of normal supermarkets. I couldn't wear clothing or shoes that my family brought. I had to purchase it inside. They are obviously overpriced. I was even charged 200 yuan [US$32] for my family to visit.

(Yuemiao, 23)

Even worse, some sex workers told me that the government officers woke them up in the early morning and forced them to get in the back of a truck wearing prisoners' uniforms. They were then paraded around the streets for everyone to see, the purpose of the parade seemingly to simply insult and humiliate them. Yet the government wants the sex worker to return to a "normal job" after she is released from the custody centre.

One night in June 2016, I went to a dark alley to meet with Siuhan. Siuhan, a streetwalker, promised to talk to me at her flat about her experience in the custody centre. When I arrived at the alley, in the dim light

I saw Siuhan at her door flirting with a customer. Her voice was sultry and sweet, full of titillation. Siuhan leaned over and invited her client to come inside. As they spoke, she realized that I was awkwardly standing nearby looking at them. I flashed a smile towards her and she gave me a friendly wink before turning back to the client to seal her deal. I had to wait another 30 minutes outside in the dark alley before Siuhan finally greeted me with a big smile. As I sat inside her apartment, Siuhan shared the same tale as Lotus.

> I have to wear a bright yellow prisoner vest, with the name badge in front of my chest. I was forced to walk along the strip of downtown [Dongguan]. My hands are tied up with handcuffs and lots of police were watching me. Of course, the police want to insult me, they included my real name, date of birth, and hometown.
>
> (Siuhan, 28)

Practical Education

Respondents also highlighted that the structured, albeit rare, "re-education"-oriented activities were not effective. While detained, many sex workers were given outdated Mao-era literature. Qiqi from Sichuan, Yuchan from Hunan, and Mary from Chongqing were all former detainees working at the low-end Peach Bar. They discussed their frustrations with what they were expected to "learn" from their custody education.

> I laughed out loud when the instructor showed me parts of the China constitution. They said sex work is a taboo in China's constitution and it is a shameful career. I was forced to memorize Maoism ... like re-education through the labour camp is a glorified honour ... Right now, who cares about Mao? Who cares about socialist doctrines in today's China?
>
> (Qiqi, 20)

> Occasionally someone would visit us and make us read about Mao's doctrines and the constitution. Most of the time, I worked in a sweatshop sewing clothes that would be shipped overseas. In the name of the government then under the façade of "Custody Education," they took advantage of me. I provided free labour for the enterprises that the police collaborated with. I had to pay about 300 yuan [US$48] living expenses per month. Next time, if the police arrest and send me to the custody centre I

would rather commit suicide … cut my wrist or bite my tongue and die in front of them. I swear I won't let any cadres get my hard-earned money.

(Yuchan, 21)

The government does not care about us; it is very obvious. It's all about money. It's neither correctional nor educational! Sometimes, they test us for STDs and see whether we are infected or not. The government does it for the safety and stability of the society but not for us. I know some girls who were detained and sent to an isolated custody centre and allowed to die. They did not provide enough medicine. The Chinese government, police, capitalists are bribing each other and run custody education centres as a business …

(Mary, 29)

The curriculum sex workers are exposed to does little to help them leave the sex industry or even provide helpful information on health and safety issues. Dingding migrated to the city as one of contemporary China's growing contingent of working girls. She reflects on her choices after leaving detention:

I was kept in the custody centre for seven months but it didn't help me change my career. After I got out of the centre I went back to sex work as soon as I could because the salary is very lucrative. The custody centre actually only benefits local cadres and the police. They took my money and cause me misery using the excuse of "education."

(Dingding, 24)

Sex Workers' Reflections: Revising the Yellow Crackdowns and Custody Education

Almost all of the participating interviewees (95 per cent) vigorously objected to how they were treated when detained. Despite the shared frustration, many also asserted that the criminalization of sex work is unlikely to change during their working lives. Although the Yellow Crackdowns have had an impact among sex workers in Dongguan, many of those interviewed still said they were willing to accept government policies that tackled and punished sex work. In some cases, this acceptance was on a superficial level; many claimed that they could get around these laws by simply bribing police with red packet money.

However, overall, many were upset with custody education and the nature of police–sex worker interactions. Suiling, from Sichuan, and Zihan, from Chongqing, both worked in the mid-tier commercial sex markets. They experienced custody education for three months and five months, respectively. Suling remarks:

> I can tolerate the government or police crackdown on us. I try to accept that they say they are doing it for the sake of common people. I am more than happy to give red packet money to the police if they warn us before they come to the bar ... what I cannot tolerate is the inhumane system of the custody centre ...
>
> (Suling, 25)

Zihan agreed with Suling and hopes the police will treat them better,

> Most people don't accept sex workers because they think we are bad women. People think we are materialistic gold diggers who try to steal husbands. We understand why the government wants to crack down on the industry; they think it will help maintain stability and peace in society. However, the Chinese government does not monitor the police, and custody education is in the hands of police.
>
> (Zihan, 26)

Zihan's point is that custody education does not have to be inherently negative for detainees. This is particularly important given that these spaces were initially conceived as rehabilitative environments. In addition to educational and moral pedagogy, these spaces are intended to provide women with sexual health-related care. The official guidelines asserted that the purpose of detention was to "maintain public order in the city," to "eradicate the parasitic population," to "liberate prostitutes," and to "provide relief" to the poor, as well as to ensure that internees "receive reform, education, and skills training" (Beijing shi minzhengju, 1949). The re-education-centre curriculum taught sex workers to equate their current "improper" occupations with victimization. Mao had long stressed that, unlike enemies of the state, who should be "forced to reform themselves through labour," the lumpenproletariat (underclass) should be "exhorted" and "persuaded," but not compelled, to join the revolution (Mao, 1926). Sex worker rehabilitation is intended to achieve this goal by using education to instil "labour skills" and "a love of labour" (Beijing shi minzhengju, 1949; Huabei minzhengbu, 1949). "[Re-educators] should follow the guiding principle of combining labour and production with political education ... to help [internees] establish a mentality of patriotic observance of law, [develop an appreciation] of the gloriousness of labour, learn labour and production skills, and cultivate the habit of loving labour, so that they become self-sufficient labourers who partici-pate in the larger socialist project" (Guowuyuan, 1957). However, these intentions and ideologies behind sex worker rehabilitative initiatives are rarely actualized. Despite the underlying aims, the day-to-day mainte-nance of these centres is often very different in practice. In effect, custody education is only a superficial effort towards stability maintenance.

Discussion and Conclusion

I have said that sex workers imprisoned in custody education embody the role of the *homo sacer*. Based on the accounts of sex workers who have served custody education sentences, it is undeniable that exploita-tion and abuse are rampant. The nature and length of the punishments administered depends almost entirely on the decisions made by indi-vidual officers. Sincere, honest, conscientious, and kind correction offi-cers are seemingly rare. Instead, abuse and violence are said to be the norm between staff and detainees. The detained sex worker, under the control of the state, is routinely exploited, assaulted, and abused, with-out repercussions. The discussion that follows focuses on three major controversial areas: the guiding principles of custody education, crimi-nal justice, and long-term impacts on social policymakers in today's China.

Upholding the Guiding Principles of Custody Education in China

The dehumanization of custody education is reinforced in various ways. Violence, abuse, harsh and inadequate living conditions, and forced labour are examples of the exploitation that sex workers must negoti-ate in the government-run institutions where they must serve. In effect, basic human rights are not afforded to the sex workers in these facili-ties. Moreover, their lack of claim to basic human rights is reinforced by their strategic physical exclusion from society through their detain-ment. Although my discussion departs from Agamben's iteration of the *homo sacer*, there are evident points of contact. Custody centres have many similarities to the refugee camps discussed by Agamben, insofar as they are spaces wherein the expectations of civil society are entirely abandoned in an effort to enforce the exclusion of the sex worker. The physical removal from civil society echoes Agamben's discussion on the role of the ban, or dead life. The sovereign-bare life resides in the zone of indistinction of inclusion/exclusion, insofar as the *homo sacer* is excluded through the ban but is included by virtue of its relationship in opposition to the sovereign (Agamben, 1998, p. 107; Spencer, 2009, p. 226). In the education centre, punishments (death, harassment) and violence (bullying, exploitation) enacted by law enforcement become instruments of bio-power that all work to affirm the lack of agency and legitimacy of the *homo sacer*. That said, by and large, most sex workers who are charged do not serve sentences. Instead, most are typically fined heavily and released upon payment. Although the Ministry of Public Security has cautioned local police not to substitute fines for detention, a lack of oversight means that local law enforcement continues to impose fines at their own discretion. Most of the sex workers pinpointed that the only reliable option to avoid detention is to offer exorbitant bribes to the police in the centre. The culture of corruption is reinforced by the fact that law enforcement relies upon the profit generated from custody education centres (Fu, 2005). At times, there will be fixed quotas for arrests and monetary demands from the department; these circumstances can lead law enforcement to make stringent efforts to arrest and detain significant numbers of sex workers. For instance, in order to meet quotas, police in Guangdong Province will occasionally organize Yellow Crackdowns for the primary purpose of replenishing jailhouse workshops or to gain revenue through harsh fines. Sex workers reflect that the state is able to punish and exploit offenders with utter disregard for their basic human rights. Their treatment and exploitation effectively position sex workers as quintessential embodiments of the *homo sacer*, in opposition to the rights-bearing, legitimate citizen.

Custody education centres and law enforcement reinforce the stigma of sex work and perpetuate exploitation and violence against sex workers. This stigmatization is further encouraged and normalized during public raids as well as by exploiting sex workers for cheap labour once they are detained. Moreover, their treatment while detained only secures their marginalized position in society (Johnson & Wang, 2018). The conditions of custody education leave little opportunity for offenders to leave the centre and take on new career and social paths. The public displays of anti-sex work sentiment normalized through mass arrests assert a notion that these attitudes are acceptable, and suggest the value of the state and law enforcement in maintaining order within the society.

As this chapter has revealed, custody education merely continues to exclude and place sex workers at the margins. There are ways to lessen the stigmatization and exploitation that sex worker detainees face. However, in order to do so, it is important to standardize punishment to make sure that some detainees are not arbitrarily given longer sentences. There is a need for mandatory training on ethical and appropriate ways of handling women during arrest and detention. Some women described the experience as dehumanizing. In addition to proper treatment, the curriculum provided to detainees must also change to one that suits their needs beyond their time in custody education. Finally, there needs to be greater oversight of the centre's daily operations. The labour of these women should not be used as a revenue stream to maintain law enforcement operations. This is not only inappropriate but also undermines the entire concept of rehabilitation. For custody education to work, the fundamental tenants of the ideologies must be respected and practised. A system of checks and balances would provide oversight to monitor law enforcement standards and practices. Without such a system in place, unsupervised authority may succumb to the temptation of using power to normalize the exploitation of offenders. This chapter has argued for building a more incisive critique of custody education and its brutal and inhumane treatment of female sex workers in post-reform China.

Securing and protecting the basic rights of detainees addresses a widespread source of discontent. The rule of law in the creation of these liminal legal spaces has received significant attention on an international level. The culture of lawlessness and violence in spaces such as custody education stands in opposition to international commitments that the Chinese government has made. Specifically, in 1997 and 1998, the government signed two major United Nations international human rights covenants, signalling China's acceptance of universal human rights standards (Liu, 2010). In 2004, the National People's Congress (NPC) amended the Constitution, writing into the document for the first time that "the state respects and guarantees human rights," signalling that human rights are a fundamental principle of China's rule of law. Taking these factors into account, there is now an urgency to reform detention spaces and protocol. Given the reports of rampant abuse and exploitation, some sort of oversight of law enforcement regarding sex workers is critical to the development of a more just and standardized approach towards detention. Arguably, building an all-round, modestly well-off (xiaokang) and harmonious society (hexieshehui) brings the stability desired by the ruling Communist Party. Criminal offenders are often employed, by the government, as examples of the acceptability of social justice and equality.

The findings presented here contribute to a wider critique about imprisonment systems within China and provide depth and texture to the discussion of the brutal and inhumane treatment of female sex workers in its post-reform society. Bracey (1986) mentioned that Confucius taught us that people were born without innate defects, and therefore their moral growth depended upon education. Educated people should protect justice and integrity. However, with hyper-materialism and the "moral vacuum" soaring in China, most people seem to have forgotten how Confucian education enlightened them.

The Criminal Justice System in Today's China

One of the major themes in this chapter is criminal justice in China; in particular, how the Chinese government and the police treat sex workers. Most of the sex workers detained in the custody centre did not have citizenship rights and were directly labelled as unwanted, dirty, and disorderly criminals. The deviant identity not only persists in the mind of the sex worker but is also reinforced by the custody centre. China's growth and development are recognized internationally, along with its political visibility under the dual influence of economic reform and globalization. However, there remain concerns about China and the suppression of human rights. These include social movements such as in Tibet, groups like Falungong, and individuals like Liu Xiaobo and his wife. There remain criticisms about China's human rights abuses and criminal justice as well as the ways in which China engages with corrupt and abusive regimes.

The involvement of governmental officials – and police in particular – in the business sectors that abuse human rights reflects only a fraction of the problem that permeates China's political and legal system, and criminal justice (Hsiu, 2009). How does the Chinese Communist Party perceive "human" rights? Who are regarded by the CCP as "humans," entitled to the enjoyment of political and civil rights? Being human is not the criterion. Not only sex workers but also HIV/AIDS carriers, the mentally ill, and political dissidents are treated as "non-persons." The CCP believes that these people pose threats to "societal security" and should be excluded from the "normal" political and legal system. As such, they are not entitled to the constitutional protection of their political and civil rights. The brutal treatment of political dissidents in China is evidenced by how the party handled the Anti-Rightist Movement, the Cultural Revolution, the June Fourth movement, and, more recently, Liu Xiaobo and his wife, Liu Xia. It is common for the CCP to strangle freedom of speech and to trample on human rights, stifle humanity, and suppress truth (Liu, 2010). The sex workers lack support or legal protection. They are typically undereducated rural migrants facing the daunting task of overcoming their victim status to get some support within the criminal justice system in post-reform China.

Confucianism has a deep influence on China's culture. To the government, cultural harmony requires that society's needs take priority over the needs of the individual. Individual freedom, as addressed in the Universal Declaration of Human Rights, remains a conceptual goal rather than a specific policy or specific set of actions. With its roots in Confucianism, the idea of social harmony may be used to justify curbing freedom of speech and other individual rights. It is commonly held that regular clients of prostitution include government officers, successful entrepreneurs, directors of listed companies, and foreign businessmen. According to the literature, it is common for cadres to have mistresses and frequent high-end bars to make business deals. The sex workers who serve these upper echelons report that the Yellow Crackdowns are merely window dressing. Similarly, the custody centre as a form of re-education is more symbol than substance. The government neither forbids its officers to buy commercial sex nor punishes them for doing so. Thus, prostitutes lack protection from the legal system. Trafficking victims and streetwalkers – usually undereducated rural migrants – typically face severe and brutal punishment by government officers once they are in the custody centres.

The Chinese penal system, in employing an extensive network of forced labour camps so as to "reform" criminals, lacks a fair judicial process. Although this neglect can be partially attributed to corruption and the opaque nature of the Chinese criminal justice system, the goal is maintaining stability and social harmony while simultaneously improving the economy to avoid chaos. Worse, as an institutional tool for the government to stifle political opposition, the penal system almost inevitably employs the use of both physical and psychological torture, and active police involvement. Analysing custody education is timely and gives Western countries a chance to know more about China's criminal justice and human rights issues. Custody education poses a challenge to some long-held fundamentals of Western legal systems.

I hope that exposing the dark side of custody centres and bringing the voices of the detained sex workers back in will bring Chinese human rights issues and their criminal justice system to international attention and put positive pressure on the Chinese government to rethink these issues. The international voices that seek to uncover and disseminate information about China's human rights issues should not be dismissed. The approach was successful in drawing attention and widespread criticism from the international community before and during the Beijing Olympics in 2008. This criticism will continue to haunt China, given its unparalleled tensions between political reform and economic pursuit. Further research should continue to examine how policymakers in China can depathologize sex work in post-reform China in order to improve conditions for hundreds of thousands of women struggling for a better life.

The Long-Term Impact on Social Policymakers

Despite numerous attempts by the Chinese government to combat prostitution and sex work, the "world's oldest profession" continues to exist and thrive. Although sex work is illegal in China, it has been impossible to abolish. Various Yellow Crackdown campaigns have had minimal effect. There were an estimated 300,000 sex workers in Dongguan, or about 10 per cent of the city's migrant population, before the Yellow Crackdown in April 2013 (Phillips, 2013). My research findings revealed that most of the detained sex workers will return to the sex work industry with its good salaries after they are released from the custody centre (Davis, 1937). The Chinese government cannot just impose a Yellow Crackdown as the guiding principle behind its policies. The government needs to improve human rights and devote more resources to setting up NGOs to help the sex workers participate in retraining programs. So far in China, there are no major formal NGOs registered to help female sex workers, but only a few relatively limited ones. There are quite a large number of NGOs helping male sex workers avoid getting infected by HIV. However, relatively few NGOs help female sex workers by providing retraining to encourage them to leave the commercial sex industry. Retraining programs have proven to be the most successful way to prevent women from moving in and out of street-based or indoor sex work. We hope that China can let the detained sex workers experience a sense of dignity and warmth by providing meaningful rehabilitation.

Understanding the New Trends in China's Commercial Sex Industry

Revisiting Dongguan in 2017 and New Developments in the Sex Work Industry

I returned to Dongguan in summer 2017 to visit the owners of each of the three venues where I had worked: the Dragon Palace, the Lotus Club, and the Peach Bar. Not surprisingly, only the Dragon Palace was still in operation. In the wake of repeated crackdowns, only the high-end club had the bargaining power and money to remain, a testament to the importance of connections and rewards in the form of the ubiquitous red packets that are so common in Chinese culture. I found that the mid-tier and low-end bars had both vanished after Spring Festival of 2017. The "old" trend for sex workers to survive was to stay in different niche markets in Dongguan. However, since the huge and severe Yellow Crackdown campaigns targeted sex workers in February 2014, the commercial sex landscape in Dongguan has changed considerably. Low-end sex services have been disproportionately and negatively affected; high-end bar owners, by contrast, have the financial resources and social capital to bribe police. The "new" trend is that after the frequent crackdowns, sex workers previously living in Dongguan have had to move to other cities, such as Hong Kong, Ningbo (Zhejiang province), and Huizhou (Guangdong province). Hong Kong is different from mainland China. Despite the numerous attempts made by the Chinese government to combat sex work, it continues to thrive. My follow-up talks indicated that many of these women continue to work from city to city as transient working girls in China. It is difficult, if not impossible, for someone outside the sex industry to maintain contact with these interviewees. Because the Yellow Crackdowns are a priority for the Chinese government in

Dongguan, sex workers must stay "hard to find." The police investigate different bars frequently and without warning.

Online Channels

In order to survive, sex work must change. Most sex workers continue to migrate to online apps such as QQ, Weibo, or Renren in order to find and maintain clients. They also use online platforms to recruit additional workers, but must be very careful and discreet. Clients can only gain access to these groups if referred or sponsored by existing clients, and membership fees must be paid up front. For example, before the girls went to Ningbo, they had already contacted the local pimps to book clients for them. This type of partner relationship mirrors those in other service industries where the work and the charges are arranged in advance. One story of note demonstrates how widespread this practice has become. Ken, the boss of the Dragon Palace, informed me that a mommy in another bar had been recently caught and on her phone the police found over 300 active Weibo groups (like WhatsApp groups). Almost all of them involved prostitution. These Weibo groups have a limit of 500 members per group and include active pimps all around China. Typically it is the sex workers who initiate contact with the pimps. More recently, because of Yellow Crackdowns, most sex workers are using online platforms like "MeMe Live" (MeMe Zhibao直播) to avoid being arrested. The Weibo/WeChat/QQ/Renren groups are really secretive and implicit so as to avoid troubles with the police. Ken told me how they use clever wording to promote and advertise girls:

> Some girls would send a message like "Beijing Retail Company, Receptionist Needed. Contact Miss Li (1997): Room E, No, 178, Xidan Lu, 4000." At first you'd think this was actually a job advertisement but what it really means is Miss Li was born in 1997 with the height of 178 cm and a bra size of E cup, a minimum service charge of 4,000 yuan [US$588]. The women won't usually contact the clients directly. Rather, they are managed by the pimps who arrange the meetings with the clients. When the worker arrives in a new city, they'd change their username so it's easier for pimps to search them up. For example: Xiao Li would change her name to "Huizhou Xiao Li" after coming to Huizhou ... They'd usually have a picture to accompany their account so the pimp can show potential clients. If the client is not a regular, they'd have to pay a deposit first. Regular clients usually pay through Alipay or WeChat wallet.

With the severe Yellow Crackdown in Dongguan, these online platforms will continue to thrive in post-socialist China.

Smelling Opportunity in Hong Kong

I met Suki, a 29-year-old mommy, in March 2017. Suki had previously worked in Dongguan during the Yellow Crackdown and had since worked in Dongguan, Ningbo, Huizhou, and Shenzhen. When I met her she was working in Hong Kong. She admitted that she knew early on that the only way to advance in the industry was to manage other sex workers, and she transitioned when she was 26. Suki is personable and outgoing and has an exceptional social network. She also has a keen sense of how to make the system work for her.

Suki arranges for girls to visit Hong Kong by capitalizing on the Individual Visit Scheme, a policy whereby residents from 49 mainland cities can visit Hong Kong for up to seven days without a visa. I spoke with a few dozen of the girls involved, who told me that they are ready to travel anywhere around the country. Some of the more popular girls bragged that they could see four or five clients a day. After one week, they simply packed up and flew somewhere else. Suki's workers are typically between 18 and 35 years old; she said that most Hong Kong sex workers are older, so her girls have an advantage. Although the girls report to Suki and pay her room rent, they find their own clients and keep 40 per cent of what they are paid.

From her share, Suki has purchased 10 apartments in Hong Kong, mainly in older buildings located in old districts like Sham Shui Po, Jordan, Yaumatei, and Sheungwan. She has renovated the apartments by creating 10 tiny rooms approximately 10 square metres in size (100 square feet). All 10 rooms share access to a single small bathroom. Altogether Suki owns over 100 tiny rooms, and she rents a room to each girl for the week for 2,000 yuan (US$295). Suki said she typically earns about 100,000 yuan (US$14,705) every month, while some girls can earn upwards of 60,000 yuan (US$8, 823) before paying the seven-days' rent to Suki.

Sex Workers as a "Floating Population"

Wherever they see opportunity is where the sex workers go. Strong relationships with local pimps are a crucial element. For instance, before sex workers come to a new city, such as Ningbo, they need to contact local pimps in order to book clients. Online communication has modernized and streamlined the process. This is preferable because of widespread anxiety that police can raid bars, particularly those that are low- and mid-tier, frequently and without warning. Lotus is still working as a streetwalker, but she updated me explaining that some girls are working in Huizhou, a small city in Guangdong that hasn't caught the attention of the Chinese government and police yet. The police there are not as intense about prosecuting sex workers as the Dongguan police. Of paramount importance is that Huizhou is not the target for the Chinese government's Yellow Crackdowns. Hence, the low-end and mid-tier sex workers can survive there. My friend Qiqi left the low-end Peach Bar and works in Huizhou. She says,

> I bought a 400-square-metre apartment in Huizhou and opened a members-only club. I hired a lot of high-quality women, and I get lots of clients who are foreigners and cadres. I am my own boss and I can control my destiny. In the past, I could never tell my parents and brothers that I am supporting them by doing sex work in the city. What do you think will happen if my parents and family members were to discover that I was a prostitute? However, right now, my parents know that I work in a hotel. Perhaps they suspect I had worked as a prostitute. But now I built three two-story villas in my hometown and my relatives are jealous of my achievement. Parents and siblings appreciate how I help them, and they don't care what I do … I can buy luxury goods.

Hyper-Materialism and the Moral Vacuum

Qiqi's conversation makes it clear that China is experiencing two troubling issues. Qiqi – like other sex workers I interviewed in Dongguan – contextualized how sex work has become socially acceptable as China's hyper-materialism is combined with its relaxing norms on sexuality. Some argue that sex work is even desirable now among the middle class as they pursue individualization, freedom, and quality of life. The consumer revolution is ubiquitous and has reshaped women's gender ideologies about the implications of becoming a sex worker. In the context of post-reform China's macro-economic reforms and its (febrile) pursuit of consumption – which is transforming the country's individualized new middle-class youth – the choices of migrant women to participate in sex work are understandable. These "choices" speak to the desire to attain money as a means of pursuing "projects of individualization" with multiple returns. Ostensibly, China's neoliberal economic reforms have been successful. They have also attenuated collective and communal bonds in the rural milieu. The sex industry exposes its practitioners to the rigours of a metropolitan economy. Post-reform Chinese society has already been penetrated by cosmopolitan imperatives that are transforming highly industrialized and risk-averse East Asian societies (Beck & Grande, 2010). As the number and complexity of the risks in East Asian societies are greater than those of the risks in European ones (Han & Shim, 2010, p. 476), novel trajectories of individualization are foreseeable across all sectors of Chinese society. It is hoped that this analysis has served as a case study in its own right and as an invitation to comparative or transnational research inside and outside the sex industry.

If their parents or siblings were told the truth about how these women were paid, there would probably be one of two outcomes. One outcome is the rationalization that the money is earned on strictly utilitarian grounds. Money sent to families would be accepted with the qualification that, although they do not condone their daughters' actions, the suffering involved in its acquisition obliges them as beneficiaries to accept and use it for strictly worthy ends. The second outcome is that they refuse the money. But by refusing to reduce or subordinate the exchange value of the money to the shameful and unethical manner of its acquisition, family members who adopt this stance are sidestepping the charge that they are depersonalizing and objectifying their daughters as commodities.

The other issue is the collapse of moral and ideological standards. The social and cultural changes brought on by China's economic growth are in turn shaping the sex workers' motives and desires. Most of the high-end sex workers come from well-to-do families whose parents are cadres, professionals, and entrepreneurs. They did not want to follow in their parents' footsteps, opting instead to pursue a relatively flexible job – as a sex worker – to escape pressure from their parents. The sex workers, particularly the high-end ones, want to escape China within the context of China's "value vacuum" (Link, Madsen, & Pickowicz, 2013). People's discontent with the lack of a uniform moral ideology in the post-reform era, following the collapse of a strong public ideology, was presented in chapter 5.

Social Policy and Criminal Justice

My book has many implications for social policymakers. Further research should continue to examine how policymakers in China can depathologize sex work in post-reform China in order to improve conditions for hundreds of thousands of women struggling for a better life. My book has offered some real-life examples of high-end sex workers in China who married clients and went on to have a stereotypically healthy, happy family life. It reveals how love heals and how love turns the sex workers' lives around. This is hopeful evidence that at least some sex workers have the right to change their job, have a family, and restart their lives. Sex workers should have opportunities to start afresh, not in factory sweatshops, sewing 140 jeans per hour, and not held back by official policies detaining them in custody centres where they essentially do the same thing. My book offers the hopeful message that sex workers can change jobs and have a good marriage and family. But the issue is complex and nuanced. Some sex workers who had opportunities to relocate overseas or in Hong Kong decided that they would rather sneak back to the commercial sex industry. One possible explanation is provided by applying the concept of edgework.

Whether or not the sex workers want to stay in the industry, the Chinese government may need to be more realistic. Since the beginning of humankind there has been sex work. It has proven difficult if not impossible to eradicate. The government may consider allocating additional funding to the NGOs to help these women. But though there are comparatively many NGOs or social organizations to help male sex workers, there are far fewer to help female sex workers change jobs, to monitor their health for sexually transmitted diseases (STDs) and HIV/AIDS, or to provide job training to those who want to exit the commercial sex industries. In general, the government invests scarce resources in female sex workers. With the research evidence presented here, I hope the Chinese government can reconsider the so-called Triple No Policy (no approval, no support, no help) towards the female sex workers.

In addition, the findings of my book will help policymakers decide how to provide retraining to the single-adult migrants and improve their working situation. This will give the migrants time to find suitable partners and even perhaps get married. Subsequently, they will no longer pose a threat to society or risk participating in social disorder via ideological movements that disrupt China's stability and harmony.

One of the major themes in my book is criminal justice; in particular, how the Chinese government and the police arrest, detain, and treat the sex workers. But consider that regular clients of prostitution have always included men of wealth and power. The sex workers who serve these upper echelons are evidence that the Yellow Crackdowns and custody centre treatment operate as a form of window dressing to mask the private behaviour of state officers. Therefore, prostitutes lack protection from the legal system. At the high end, sex workers facilitate emotional labour and serve officials. But low- and mid-tier sex workers face severe and brutal punishment from crackdowns and detention in the government custody centres.

To unveil and expose the dark side of the custody centres and give voice to the detained sex workers, positive dialogue must begin about human rights issues and the criminal justice system. It is the only way for the system to improve. The international voices that help to uncover and disseminate information about China's human rights issues should not be dismissed.

Limitations of the Book

For the time being, this particular research journey has come to an end. Hopefully, other exciting journeys await. The work here has truly turned out to be a learning process – the subject matter, the actual research work, and, most certainly, the trials and tribulations of writing it. To paraphrase Ceglowski (1997): If I could redo the study, I might well have done it differently – or not, as the case may be. Everything could have been done differently in hindsight, had I more time and resources.

There is, however, a need to address some of the limitations of the research and future research themes. First, the research focused only in Dongguan, Guangdong; it would be more comprehensive to focus on some of the other cities such as Shanghai, Beijing, second-tier cities like Wuhan and Chengdu, and some coastal regions besides Guangdong, to avoid homogenous findings. Although Dongguan is a valuable field site, it is undeniable that China's commercial sex industry fluctuates from city to city, province to province. Second, more research is needed on how sex workers implement their exit plans and post-marriage life. Most of the respondents I met five and even seven years ago have moved to other cities and countries. This transience made it impossible to follow them via WeChat or other social media platforms. I don't have enough data to present their post-marriage life within China or outside China. Future research may focus more on this topic.

In sum, it was enlightening for me to see the humanity of these brave women who have overcome countless hurdles to secure a life. They have negotiated dangerous and sometimes violent conditions yet remain resolute and determined to be free, as they understand freedom. They look in the mirror each day and see a smart, savvy, successful woman in a world that tries not to recognize them. To me, they are the true champions.

References

Agamben, G. (1998). *Homo sacer: Sovereign power and bare life* (D. Heller-Roazen, Trans.). Stanford: Stanford University Press.

Allison, A. (1994). *Nightwork: Sexuality, pleasure, and corporate masculinity in a Tokyo hostess club*. Chicago: University of Chicago Press.

Asia Catalyst. (2013). Custody and education: Arbitrary detention for female sex workers in China. Beijing:1–48. Retreived https://www.nswp.org/sites/nswp.org/files/AsiaCatalyst_CustodyEducation2013-12-EN.pdf

Askew, M. (2002). *Bangkok: Place, practice and representation*. London: Routledge.

Barbezat, S.M. (2009). *Trafficking of women and the harmonious society: The Chinese national plan of action on combating trafficking in women and children*. Retrieved September 9, from https://www.du.edu/korbel/hrhw/researchdigest/china/China.pdf

Batchelor, S.A. (2007). Getting mad wi'it': Risk-seeking by young women. In K. Hannah-Moffat & P. O'Malley (Eds.), *Gendered risks* (pp. 205–27). Abingdon: Routledge & Cavendish.

Beck, U., & Grande, E. (2010). Varieties of second modernity: The cosmopolitan turn in social and political theory and research. *British Journal of Sociology, 61*(3), 409–43.

Beck, U., & Ritter, M. (1992). *Risk society: Towards a new modernity*. London: Sage Publications.

Beijing shi minzhengju [Beijing Municipal Bureau of Civil Affairs]. (1949). Beiping shi chuli jinü banfa, caoan [Beiping municipality regulations for the management of prostitutes, draft measure]. Beijing Municipal Archives, 196-2-20.

Bernstein, E. (1999). What's wrong with prostitution? What's right with sex work? Comparing markets in female sexual labour. *Hastings Women's Law Journal, 10*(1), 91–117.

Bernstein, E. (2007). *Temporarily yours: Intimacy, authenticity, and the commerce of sex*. Chicago: University of Chicago Press.

Bernstein, E. (2008). Sexual commerce and the global flow of bodies, desires, and social policies. *Sexuality Research and Social Policy, 5*(4), 1–15.

Bourdieu, P. (1977). *Outline of a theory of practice.* Cambridge: Cambridge University Press.

Bourdieu, P. (1984). *Distinction: A social critique of the judgment of taste.* Cambridge, MA: Harvard University Press.

Bourdieu, P. (1986). The forms of capital. In J. Richardson (Ed.), *Handbook of theory and research for the sociology of education* (pp. 241–58). New York: Greenwood.

Bracey, D.H. (1986). The system of justice and the concept of human nature in the People's Republic of China. *Justice Quarterly, 2*(1), 139–44.

Brennan, D. (2004). *What's love got to do with it? Transnational desires and sex tourism in the Dominican Republic.* Durham, NC: Duke University Press.

Brents, B. (2017). *Working paper on sex work/trafficking.* Retrieved March 24, 2017, from http://faculty.washington.edu/lerum/8-Sex-Work-Trafficking.pdf

Brents, B.G., & Jackson, C.A. (2013). Gender, emotional labour, and interactive body work: Negotiating flesh and fantasy in sex workers' labor practices. In C. Wolkowitz, R.L. Cohen, T. Sanders, and K. Hardy (Eds.), *Body/sex/work* (pp. 77–92). Basingstoke: Palgrave Macmillan.

Brown, E. (2007). *The ties that bind: Migration and trafficking of women and girls for sexual exploitation in Cambodia.* Phnom Penh: International Organization for Migration.

Brown, M.E. (1978). Teenage prostitution. *Adolescence, 14,* 665–680.

Brown, P., & Levinson, S. (1987). *Politeness: Some universals in language usage.* Cambridge: Cambridge University Press.

Busza, J. (2004). Sex work and migration: The dangers of oversimplification: A case study of Vietnamese women in Cambodia. *Health and Human Rights, 7*(2), 231–49.

Butler, J. (1993). *Bodies that matter: On the discursive limits of "sex".* New York: Routledge.

Ceglowski, D. (1997). That's a good story, but is it really research? *Qualitative Inquiry, 3*(2), 188–201.

Chan, K.W. (2012). Internal labor migration in China: Trends, geography and policies. In *United Nations population division, population distribution, urbanization, internal migration and development: An international perspective* (pp. 81–102). New York: United Nations.

Chan, W., & Rigakos, G.S. (2002). Risk, crime and gender. *British Journal of Criminology, 42*(4), 743–61.

Chapkis, W. (1997). *Live sex acts: Women performing erotic labor.* New York: Routledge.

Chen, M.H. (2017). Crossing borders to buy sex: Taiwanese men negotiating gender, class and nationality in the Chinese sex industry. *Sexualities, 20*(8), 921–94.

Cheng, S. (2012). *On the move for love*. Philadelphia: Pennsylvania University Press.

Chesley, N. (2011). Stay-at-home fathers and breadwinning mothers: Gender, couple dynamics, and social change. *Gender & Society, 25*(5), 642–64.

Chin, C. (2013). *Cosmopolitan sex workers*. Oxford: Oxford University Press.

China Daily. (2010, May 22). China plans draft immigration law. Retrieved August 31, 2015, from http://www.chinadaily.com.cn/china/2010-05/22/content_9881622.html

China Daily. (2014, March 28). China's top 10 cities for salaries. Retrieved October 29, 2017, from http://www.chinadaily.com.cn/business/201403/28/content_17383764_10.htm

China Statistical Yearbook. (2005). Beijing: China Statistics Press. Retrieved July 5, 2016, from http://www.stats.gov.cn/tjsj/ndsj/2005/indexeh.htm

Choi, S.Y.P. (2011). State control, female prostitution and HIV prevention in China. *China Quarterly, 205*, 96–114.

Choi, S.Y.P. (2016). Gendered pragmatism and subaltern masculinity in China: Peasant men's responses to their wives' labor migration. *American Behavioral Scientist, 60*(5–6), 565–82.

Choi, S.Y.P., & Holyroyd, E. (2007). The influence of power, poverty and agency on condom negotiation among female sex workers in Mainland China. *Culture, Health and Sexuality, 9*(5), 489–503.

Choi, S.Y.P., & Luo, M. (2016). Performative family: Homosexuality, marriage and intergenerational dynamics in China. *British Journal of Sociology, 67*(2), 260–80.

Choi, S.Y.P., & Peng, Y. (2015). Humanized management? Capital and labor at a time of labor shortage in South China. *Human Relations, 68*(2), 287–304.

Cohen, E. (1986). Lovelorn *farangs*: The correspondence between foreign men and Thai girls. *Anthropological Quarterly, 59*(3), 115–27.

Connell, R.W. (1995). *Masculinities*. Berkeley: University of California Press.

Connell, R.W. (1998). Masculinities and globalization. *Men and Masculinities, 1*(1), 3–23.

Connell, R.W. (2016) Masculinities in global perspective: Hegemony, contestation, and changing structures of power. *Theory and Society 45*(4), 303–18.

Connell, R.W., & Messerschmidt, J.W. (2005). Hegemonic masculinity: Rethinking the concept. *Gender and Society, 19*(6), 829–59.

Cowen, D., & Siciliano, A. (2011) Surplus masculinities and security. *Antipode 43*(5), 1513–61.

Craig, J.F., & Fournet, L. (1987). A typology of office harlots: Mistresses, party girls, and career climbers. *Deviant Behavior, 8*(4), 319–28.

Crenshaw, K. (1991). Mapping the margins: Intersectionality, identity politics, and violence against women of color. *Stanford Law Review, 43*, 1241–99.

Cressy, P.G. (2008). *The taxi-dance hall: A sociological study in commercialized recreation and city life*. Chicago: University of Chicago Press.

Cunningham, S., & Kendall, T.D. (2011). Prostitution 2.0: The changing face of sex work. *Journal of Urban Economics, 69*(3), 273–87.

Davies, K. (2013, January). *China investment policy: An update, OECD working papers on international investment*. OECD Publishing. Retrieved from http://dx.doi.org/10.1787/5k469l1hmvbt-en

Davis, K. (1937). The sociology of prostitution. *American Sociological Review, 2*(5), 744–55.

Dean, M. (2010). *Governmentality, power and rule in modern society*. London: Sage Publications.

DeCaroli, S. (2007). Boundary stones: Giorgio Agamben and the field of sovereignty. In M. Calarco & S. DeCaroli (Eds.), *Giorgio Agamben: Sovereignty and life* (pp. 43–69). Stanford: Stanford University Press.

Deflem, M. (2003). The sociology of money: Simmel and the contemporary battle of the classics. *Journal of Classical Sociology, 3*(1), 67–96.

Delph, E.W. (1978). *The silent community: Public homosexual encounters*. Beverly Hills, CA: Sage Publications.

Ding, Y., & Ho, S.Y. (2013). Sex work in China's Pearl River Delta: Accumulating sexual capital as a life-advancement strategy. *Sexualities, 16*(1–2), 43–60.

Drucker, J., & Nieri, T. (2016). Female online sex workers' perceptions of exit from sex work. *Deviant Behavior, 39*(1), 1–19.

Duneier, M. (2011). How not to lie with ethnography. *Sociological Methodology, 41*, 1–11.

Elmhirst, R. (2007). Tigers and gangsters: Masculinities and feminized migration in Indonesia. *Population, Space and Place, 13*(3), 225–38.

Fan, C.C. (2008). *China on the move: Migration, the state, and the household*. Los Angeles: University of California Press.

Faugier, J., & Sargeant, M. (1997). Sampling hard to reach populations. *Journal of Advanced Nursing, 26*, 790–7.

Ferrell, J. (2005). *Empire of scrounge: Inside the urban underground of dumpster diving, trash picking, and street scavenging*. New York: New York University Press.

Ferrell, J., Milovanovic, D., & Lyng, S. (2001). Edgework, media practices, and the elongation of meaning: A theoretical ethnography of the Bridge Day event. *Theoretical Criminology 5*(2), 177–202.

Foucault, M. (1982). The subject and power. In H.L. Dreyfus & P. Rabinow (Eds.), *Michel Foucault: Beyond structuralism and hermeneutics* (pp. 208–26). New York: Harvester Wheatsheaf.

Foucault, M. (1988). Technologies of the self. In H. Gutman, P.H. Hutton, & L.H. Martin (Eds.), *Technologies of the self: A seminar with Michel Foucault* (pp. 16–49). Amherst, MA: University of Massachusetts Press.

Foucault, M. (1990). *The history of sexuality. Volume I: An introduction* (R. Hurley, Trans.). New York: Vintage Books.

Frank, K. (1998). The production of identity and the negotiation of intimacy in a "gentleman's club". *Sexualities, 1*(2), 175–201.

Frank, K. (2002). *G-strings and sympathy: Strip club regulars and male desire.* Durham, NC: Duke University Press.

Frank, K. (2013). *Plays well in groups: A journey through the world of group sex.* Lanham, MD: Rowman & Littlefield.

Frohmann, L. (1991). Discrediting victims' allegations of sexual assault: Prosecutorial accounts of case rejection. *Social Problems, 38*(2), 213–26.

Fu, H.L. (2005). Punishing for profit: Profitability and rehabilitation in a *laojiao* institution. In N. Diamant, S.B. Lubman, & K.J. O'Brien (Eds.), *Engaging the law in China: State, society, and possibilities for justice* (pp. 213–30). Stanford: Stanford University Press.

Fuller, N. (2001). The social construction of gender identity among Peruvian men. *Men and Masculinities, 3*(3), 316–31.

Garot, R. (2015). Gang-banging as edgework. *Dialect Anthropology, 39,* 151–63.

Gilmore, D.D. (1990). *Manhood in the making: Cultural concepts of masculinity.* New Haven & London: Yale University Press.

Gimlin, D. (2007). What is body work? A review of the literature. *Sociology Compass, 1*(1), 353–70.

Glenn, E.N. (2008). Yearning for lightness: Transnational circuits in the marketing and consumption of skin lighteners. *Gender and Society, 22*(3), 281–302.

Goffman, E. (1972). On face-work: An analysis of ritual elements in social interaction. In E. Goffman (Ed.), *Interaction ritual: Essays on face-to-face behaviour* (pp. 5–46). London: Penguin.

Goldstein, P.J. (1982). Occupational mobility in the world of prostitution: Becoming a madam. *Deviant Behavior, 4*(3–4), 267–79.

Guowuyuan [State Council]. (1957). Guowuyuan guanyu laodong jiaoyang wenti de jueding [Decision of the State Council regarding the question of re-education through labour]. In *Zhonghua renmin gongheguo fagui huibian* (Vol. 6, pp. 243–4). Beijing: Zhongguo fazhi chubanshe.

Hail-Jares, K., Choi, S., Duo, L., Luo, Z., & Huang, Z.J. (2016). Occupational and demographic factors associated with drug use among female sex workers at the China-Myanmar border. *Drug Alcohol Dependence, 161,* 42–9.

Halperin, D. (2007). *How to do the history of homosexuality* (1st ed.). Chicago: University of Chicago Press.

Ham, J., & Gilmour, F. (2016). "We all have one": Exit plans as a professional strategy in sex work. *Work, Employment and Society, 31*(5), 1–16.

Hamilton, A. (1997). Primal dream: Masculinism, sin and salvation in Thailand's sex trade. In L. Manderson & M. Jolly (Eds.), *Sites of desire/ economies of pleasure: Sexualities in Asia and the Pacific* (pp. 145–65). Chicago: University of Chicago Press.

Han, S.J., & Shim, Y.H. (2010). Redefining second modernity for East-Asia: A critique assessment. *British Journal of Sociology, 61*(3), S465–88.

Hansen, M.H. (2014). *The individualization of Chinese state education: Life in a rural boarding school.* Seattle: University of Washington Press.

He, H. (2014, April 7). Crackdown on Dongguan sex trade leaves wider economy in slump. *South China Morning Post.* Retrieved October 26, 2014, from http://www.scmp.com/news/china/article/1466356/crackdown-dongguan-sex-trade-leaves-wider-economy-slump

Ho, W.C. (2014). Biopolitics, occupational health and state power: The marginalization of sick workers in China. *China Quarterly, 219*(September), 808–26.

Hoang, K.K. (2010). Economies of emotion, familiarity, fantasy, and desire: Emotional labour in Ho Chi Minh City's sex industry. *Sexualities, 13*(2), 255–72.

Hoang, K.K. (2011). "She's not a low class dirty girl": Sex work in Ho Chi Minh City, Vietnam. *Journal of Contemporary Ethnography, 40*(4), 367–96.

Hoang, K.K. (2014a). Competing technologies of embodiment: Pan-Asian modernity and third world dependency in Vietnam's contemporary sex industry. *Gender and Society, 28*(4), 513–36.

Hoang, K.K. (2014b). Vietnam rising dragon: Contesting dominant Western masculinities in Ho Chi Minh City's global sex industry. *International Journal of Politics, Culture and Society, 27*(2), 259–71.

Hoang, K.K. (2015). *Dealing in desire: Asian ascendancy, Western decline, and the hidden currencies of global sex work.* Oakland: University of California Press.

Hoang, L.A., & Yeoh, B.S.A. (2011). Breadwinning wives and "left-behind" husbands: Men and masculinities in the Vietnamese transnational family. *Gender & Society, 25*(6), 717–39.

Hochschild, A.R. (2003/1983). *The managed heart: Commercialization of human feeling.* Berkeley: University of California Press.

Hoefinger, H. (2011). Professional girlfriends. *Cultural Studies, 25*(2), 244–66.

Hoefinger, H. (2013). *Sex, love and money: Professional girlfriends and transactional relationships in Cambodia.* Abingdon: Routledge.

Hsiu, L.T. (2009). *Human rights in China Fall 2009.* Retrieved September 9, 2017, from https://www.du.edu/korbel/hrhw/researchdigest/china/China.pdf

Hsu, C.L. (2005). A taste of "modernity": Working in a Western restaurant in market socialist China. *Ethnography, 6*(4), 543–65.

Huabei minzhengbu [North China Ministry of Civil Affairs]. (1949). Chuli qigai zanxing banfa [Provisional regulations for the management of beggars]. Beijing Municipal Archives, 196-2-191.

Huang, J. (2015). *Will more children save China?* Retrieved October 17, 2017, from http://www.womenofchina.cn/html/features/15122198-1.htm

Huang, Y.Y., Manman, S., & Pan, S. (2012). Understanding the diversity of male clients of sex workers in China and the implications for HIV prevention programs. *Global Public Health, 7*(5), 509–21.

Human Rights Watch. (2013). *"Swept away": Abuses against sex workers in China.* Retrieved May 30, 2018, from https://www.refworld.org/docid/519b1ee74.html

Hunter, A. (2005). *Respect sex workers' human rights: Stop all violence against sex workers.* Hong Kong: Network of Sex Work Projects. Retrieved June 1, 2017, from https://www.nswp.org/sites/nswp.org/files/Respect%20All%20Sex%20Workers%20Rights%20December%2017%202005.pdf

Huschke, S., & Schubotz, D. (2016). Commercial sex, clients, and Christian morals: Paying for sex in Ireland. *Sexualities, 19*(7), 869–87.

Jabbar, N. (2011). B.R. Ambedkar's challenge to the Puranic past. *Postcolonial Studies, 14*(1), 23–43.

Jabbar, N. (2012). Policing native pleasures: A colonial history. *British Journal of Sociology, 63*(4), 704–29.

Jacka, T. (2009). *Gender and labour migration in Asia.* Geneva: IOM International Organization for Migration.

Jacka, T. (2012). Migration, householding and the well-being of left-behind women in rural Ningxia. *China Journal, 67*, 1–22.

James, J., & Meyerding, J. (1977). Early sexual experience and prostitution. *American Journal of Psychiatry, 134*(1), 1381–5.

Jankowiak, W., Gray, P., & Hattman, K. (2008). Globalizing evolution: Female choice, nationality, and perception of "sexual beauty" in China. *Journal of Cross-Cultural Research 10*, 1–22, 248–69.

Jankowiak, W., & Paladino, T. (2008). Desiring sex, longing for love: A tripartite conundrum. In William R. Jankowiak (Ed.), *Intimacies: Love and sex across cultures.* New York: Columbia University Press.

Jeffrey, L.A., & MacDonald, G. (2006). *Sex workers in the Maritimes talk back.* Vancouver: UBC Press.

Jeffreys, E. (2007). Governing buyers of sex in the People's Republic of China. *Economy and Society, 35*(4), 571–93.

Jeffreys, E. (2010). Exposing police corruption and malfeasance: China's virgin prostitute cases. *China Journal, 63*, 127–49.

Jeffreys, E. (2012). *Prostitution scandals in China: Policy, media and society.* Abingdon: Routledge.

Johnson, T.M., & Wang, Y.R. (2018). "Hidden identities": Perceptions of sexual identity in Beijing. *British Journal of Sociology, 69*(2), 323–51.

Joseph, J. (2012). *The social in the global: Social theory, governmentality and global politics.* Cambridge: Cambridge University Press.

Kam, L. (2002). *Chinese masculinities in a globalizing world*. Cambridge: Cambridge University Press.

Kavanaugh, P.R. (2015). The social organization of masculine violence in nighttime leisure scenes. *Criminal Justice Studies: A Critical Journal of Crime, Law and Society, 28*(3), 239–56.

Kim, J. (2015). From "country bumpkins" to "tough workers": The pursuit of masculinity among male factory workers in China. *Anthropological Quarterly, 88*(1), 133–62.

Kimmel, M.S. (1994). Masculinity as homophobia: Fear, shame and silence in the construction of gender identity. In H. Brod & M. Kaufman (Eds.), *Theorizing masculinities* (pp. 117–41). Thousand Oaks, CA: Sage Publications.

Kipnis, A. (Ed.). (2012). *Chinese modernity and the individual psyche*. Basingstoke: Palgrave Macmillan.

Klinger, K. (2003). Prostitution, humanism and a woman's choice. *Humanist, 63*(1), 16–19.

Kong, T.S.K. (2015a). Buying sex as edgework: Hong Kong male clients in commercial sex. *British Journal of Criminology, 55*, 1–18.

Kong, T.S.K. (2015b). Romancing the boundary: Client masculinities in the Chinese sex industry. *Culture, Health & Sexuality, 17*(7), 810–24.

Kong, T.S.K. (2016, July 13). Sex and work on the move: Money boys in post-socialist China. *Urban Studies*. Published online first.

Laner, M.R. (1974). Prostitution as an illegal vocation: A sociological overview. In C. Bryant (Ed.), *Deviant behavior: Occupational and organizational bases* (pp. 177–205). Chicago: Rand McNally.

Lau, Y., & Wong, D. (2008). Are concern for face and willingness to seek help correlated to early postnatal depressive symptoms among Hong Kong Chinese women? A cross-sectional questionnaires survey. *International Journal of Nursing Studies, 45*, 51–64.

Lee, C.K. (1998). *Gender and the South China Miracle: Two worlds of factory women*. Oakland: University of California Press.

Lee, C.K. (2007). The unmaking of the Chinese working class in the Northeastern Rustbelt. In C.K. Lee (Ed.), *Working in China: Ethnographies of labor and workplace transformation* (pp. 15–37). London: Routledge.

Lee, C.K., & Shen, Y. (2009). China: The paradox and possibility of a public sociology of labour. *Work and Occupations, 36*(2), 110–25.

Lee, E.S. (1966). A theory of migration. *Demography, 3*(1), 47–57.

Link, P., Madsen, R.P., & Pickowicz, P.G. (2013). *Restless China*. New York: Rowman & Littlefield.

Liu, M. (2012). Chinese migrant women in the sex industry: Exploring their paths to prostitution. *Feminist Criminology, 7*(4), 327–49.

Liu, X. (2010). *I have no enemies: My final statement* (J. Latourelle, Trans.). Retrieved July 13, 2017, from http://www.hrichina.org/en/content/3208

Lois, J. (2005). Gender and emotion management in the stages of edgework. In S. Lyng (Ed.), *Edgework: The sociology of risk-taking* (pp. 117–52). New York: Routledge.

Lovell, T. (2000). Thinking feminism with and against Bourdieu. *Feminist Theory, 1*, 11–32. doi: 10.1177/14647000022229047.

Lowe, J., & Tsang, Y.H. (2017). Disunited in ethnicity: The racialization of Chinese Mainlanders in Hong Kong. *Patterns of Prejudice, 51*(2), 137–58.

Lucas, A.M. (2005). The work of sex work: Elite prostitutes' vocational orientations and experiences. *Deviant Behavior, 26*(6), 513–46.

Lyng, S. (1990). Edgework: A social psychological analysis of voluntary risk taking. *American Journal of Sociology, 95*, 851–86.

Lyng, S. (Ed.). (2005). *Edgework: The sociology of risk-taking*. Abingdon: Routledge.

Lyng, S., & Matthews, R. (2007). Risk, edgework, and masculinities. In K. Hannah-Moffat & P. O'Malley (Eds.), *Gendered risks* (pp. 75–97). Abingdon: Routledge & Cavendish.

Mac an Ghaill, M., & Haywood, C. (2007). *Gender, culture and society: Contemporary masculinities and femininities*. Basingstoke: Palgrave Macmillan.

Mahdavi, P. (2011). *Gridlock: Labor, migration, and human trafficking in Dubai*. Palo Alto: Stanford University Press.

Mallee, H. (2003). Migration, *hukou* and resistance in reform China. In J.E. Perry & M. Selden (Eds.), *Chinese society, change, conflict and resistance* (pp. 143–60). London & New York: Routledge & Curzon.

Månsson, S.A., & Hedin, U.C. (1999). Breaking the Matthew effect on women leaving prostitution. *International Journal of Social Welfare, 8*, 67–77.

Mao, Z. (1926). Zhongguo nongmin zhong ge jieji de fenxi ji qi duiyu gemingde taidu [An analysis of the various classes among the Chinese peasantry and their attitudes toward the revolution]. Trans. in Schram and Hodes (1992), vol. 2, pp. 303–9.

McClintock, A. (1995). *Imperial leather: Race, gender, and sexuality in the colonial contest*. London: Routledge.

McDowell, L. (2003). Masculine identities and low-paid work: Young men in urban labour markets. *International Journal of Urban and Regional Research, 27*(4), 828–48.

McKeganey, N., & Barnard, M. (1996). *Sex work on the streets: Prostitutes and their clients*. London: Open University Press.

Mears, A. (2014). Aesthetic labor for the sociologies of work, gender, and beauty. *Sociology Compass, 8*(12), 1330–43. http://dx.doi.org/10.1111/soc4.12211

Miller, E.E. (1982). Prison industries in the People's Republic of China. *Prison Journal, 62*(2), 52–7.

Miller, E.M. (1986). *Street woman*. Philadelphia: Temple University Press.

Miller, E.M. (1991). Assessing the inattention to class, race/ethnicity and gender: Comment on Lyng. *American Journal of Sociology, 96*, 1530–4.

Miller, W.J. (2005). Adolescents on the edge: The sensual side of delinquency. In S. Lyng (Ed.), *Edgework: The sociology of risk-taking* (pp. 153–71). London: Routledge.

Milrod, C., & Weitzer, R. (2012). The intimacy prism: Emotion management among the clients of escorts. *Men and Masculinities, 15*(5), 447–67.

Moon, D. (2015). Review of the book *Sexual fields: Toward a sociology of collective sexual life*, by Adam Isaiah Green. *American Journal of Sociology, 120*(4), 1271–4.

National Bureau of Statistics of China. (2004–16). *Chinese labor statistical year book (2004–2016)*. Beijing: China Statistics Press.

National Bureau of Statistics of China. (2008). Retrieved September 18, 2015, from http://www.stats.gov.cn/english/StatisticalCommuniqu/

Newmahr, S. (2011). *Playing on the edge: Sadomasochism, risk, and intimacy.* Bloomington: Indiana University Press.

Nicholls, C.M. (2009). Agency, transgression and the causation of homelessness: A contextualised rational action analysis. *European Journal of Housing Policy, 9*, 69–84.

Osburg, J. (2013). *Anxious wealth: Money and morality among China's new rich.* Stanford: Stanford University Press.

Oselin, S. (2009). Leaving the streets: Transformation of prostitute identity within the Prostitution Rehabilitation Program. *Deviant Behavior, 30*(4), 379–406.

Oselin, S. (2010). Weighing the consequences of a deviant career: Motivations and opportunities for leaving prostitution. *Sociological Perspectives, 53*(4), 527–49.

Otis, E. (2011). *Markets and bodies: Women, service work and the making of inequality in China*. Stanford: Stanford University Press.

Pan, S. (1999). *Cun zai yu huang miu: Zhongguo di xia "xing chan ye" kao cha* [*Reality and absurdity: An investigation of the underground sex industry in China*]. Beijing: Qunyan Publishing House (available only in Chinese).

Pan, S. (2000). *Sheng cun yu ti yan: dui yi ge di xia "hong deng qu" de zhui zong kao cha* [*Subsistence and experience: Investigation of an underground red-light district*]. Beijing: Zhongguo shehui kexue Publishing House (available only in Chinese).

Parker, J., & Stanworth, H. (2005). "Go for it"! Towards a critical realist approach to voluntary risktaking. *Health, Risk & Society, 7*(4), 319–36.

Parreñas, R.S. (2005). *Children of global migration: Transnational families and gendered woes*. Stanford: Stanford University Press.

Parreñas, R.S. (2011a). The indentured mobility of migrant women: How gendered protectionist laws lead Filipina hostesses to forced sexual labor. *Journal of Workplace Rights, 15*(3–4), 327–39.

Parreñas, R.S. (2011b). *Illicit flirtations*. Palo Alto: Stanford University Press.

Peng, Y.W. (2007). Buying sex: Domination and difference in the discourses of Taiwanese piao-ke. *Men and Masculinities, 9*(3), 315–36.

Pheterson, G. (1989). *A vindication of the rights of whores*. Seattle: Seal Press.

Phillips, T. (2013, May 1). Inside Dongguan, China's Sin City. *Telegraph*. Retrieved September 4, 2014, from http://www.telegraph.co.uk/news/ worldnews/asia/china/10030014/Inside-Dongguan-Chinas-Sin-City.html

Pierson, C. (2011). *The modern state*. Abingdon: Routledge.

Pun, N. (2005). *Made in China: Women factory workers in a global workplace*. Durham, NC: Duke University Press.

Pun, N. (2016). *Migrant labor in China: Post-socialist transformations*. Cambridge: Polity Press.

Rajah, V. (2007). Resistance as edgework in violent intimate relationships of drug-involved women. *British Journal of Criminology, 47*(2), 196–213.

Ravenstein, E.G. (1885). The lows of migration. *Journal of the Statistical Society of London, 47*(2), 167–235.

Riessman, C.K. (1993). *Narrative analysis*. Newbury Park, CA: Sage Publications.

Rivers-Moore, M. (2013). Affective sex: Beauty, race and nation in the sex industry. *Feminist Theory, 14*(2), 153–69. http://dx.doi.org/10.1177/1464700113483242

Rivers-Moore, M. (2016). *Gringo gulch sex, tourism, and social mobility in Costa Rica*. Chicago: University of Chicago Press.

Rofel, L. (2007). *Desiring China: Experiments in neoliberalism, sexuality, and public culture*. Durham, NC: Duke University Press.

Rosen, E., & Venkatesh, S.A. (2008). A "perversion" of choice: Sex work offers just enough in Chicago's urban ghetto. *Journal of Contemporary Ethnography, 37*(4), 417–41.

Sanchez, L.E. (2004). The global Erotic Subject, the ban, and the prostitute-free zone: Sex work and the theory of differential exclusion. *Environmental and Planning D: Society and Space, 22*, 861–83.

Sanders, T. (2007). Becoming an ex-sex worker: Making transitions out of a deviant career. *Feminist Criminology, 2*(1), 1–22.

Sanders, T. (2008a). Male sexual scripts: Intimacy, sexuality and pleasure in the purchase of commercial sex. *Sociology, 42*, 400–17.

Sanders, T. (2008b). *Paying for pleasure: Men who buy sex*. Cullompton, Devon: Willan.

Sassatelli, R. (2000). From value to consumption: A social theoretical perspective on Simmel's *philosophie des geldes*. *Acta Sociologica, 43*(3), 207–18.

Savarese, J.L. (2010). "Doing no violence to the sentence imposed": Racialized sex worker complaints, racialized offenders, and the feminization of the *homo sacer* in two sexual assault cases. *Canadian Journal of Women and the Law, 22*(2), 365–95.

Schram, S.R., & Hodes, N.J. (1992). *Mao's road to power: Revolutionary writings 1912–1949*. Armonk, NY: M.E. Sharpe.

Shen, H.H. (2008, March). The purchase of transnational intimacy: Women's bodies, transnational masculine privileges in Chinese economic zones. *Asian Studies Review, 32*, 57–75.

Short, J.F. (1984). The social fabric at risk: Toward the social transformation of risk analysis. *American Sociological Review, 49*(6), 711–25.

Simon, H.A. (1955). A behavioral model of rational choice. *Quarterly Journal of Economics, 69*(1), 99–118.

Simon, H.A. (1956, March). Rational choice and the structure of the environment. *Psychological Review, 63*, 261–73.

Singer, B., & Ryff, C.D. (2001). Person-centered methods for understanding aging: The integration of numbers and narratives. In R.H. Binstock & L.K. George (Eds.), *Handbook of aging and the social sciences* (pp. 44–65). San Diego: Academic.

Smith, A.M. (2012). The dilemma of thought reform: Beijing reformatories and the origins of reeducation through labor, 1949–1957. *Modern China, 39*(2), 203–34.

Song, G., & Hird, D. (2013). *Men and masculinities in contemporary China.* Leiden: Brill.

Spence, J.D. (1996, December 19). The risks of witness [Review of the book *Troublemaker: One man's crusade against China's cruelty*, by H. Wu & G. Vecsey]. *New York Review of Books*, 1–5.

Spencer, D. (2009). Sex offender as homo sacer. *Punishment & Society, 11*(2), 219–40.

Spivak, G.C. (1995). Can the subaltern speak? Colonial discourse and post-colonial theory. In P. Williams & L. Chrisman (Eds.). *A reader* (pp. 67–109). New York: Columbia University Press.

Stanko, E. (1997). Safety talk: Conceptualizing women's risk assessment as a "technology of the soul." *Theoretical Criminology, 1*(4), 479–99.

Stoler, A. (2002). *Carnal knowledge and imperial power: Race and the intimate in colonial rule.* Berkeley: University of California Press.

Tian, X.L., & Deng, Y.X. (2017). Organizational hierarchy, deprived masculinity, and confrontational practices: Men doing women's jobs in a global factory. *Journal of Contemporary Ethnography, 46*(4), 464–89.

Tichenor, V. (2005). Maintaining men's dominance: Negotiating identity and power when she earns more. *Sex Roles, 53*(3–4), 191–205.

Trotter, H. (2008). *Sugar girls and seamen: A journey into the world of dockside prostitution in South Africa.* Athens: Ohio University Press.

Tsang, E.Y.H. (2014). *The new middle class in China: Consumption, politics and the market economy.* Frontier Globalization Series. London: Palgrave Macmillan.

Tsang, E.Y.H. (2017a, June). Neither "bad" nor "dirty": High-end sex work and intimate relationships in urban China. *China Quarterly, 230*, 444–63.

Tsang, E.Y.H. (2017b). Finding hope as a "tempting girl" in China: Sex work, indentured mobility, and cosmopolitan individuals. *Deviant Behavior, 38*(8), 1–14.

Tsang, E.Y.H. (2018a, February). Real men get the best bar girls: Performing masculinities in China's global sex industry. *Deviant Behavior*, 1–15. Online version first.

Tsang, E.Y.H. (2018b, March). Erotic authenticity: Comparing intimate relationships between high-end bars and low-end bars in China's global sex industry. *Deviant Behavior*, 1–15. Online version first.

Tsang, E.Y.H. (2019). Selling sex as an edgework: Risk taking and thrills in China's commercial sex industry. *International Journal of Offender Therapy and Comparative Criminology*. http://doi:10.1177/0306624X18818925. Online version first.

Tsang, E.Y.H., Lowe, J., Scambler, G., & Wilkinson, J. (2018). Peasant sex workers in metropolitan China and the pivotal concept of money: A sociological investigation. *Asian Journal of Social Science, 46*(2), 358–79.

Tulloch, J., & Lupton, D. (2003). *Risk and everyday life*. London: Sage Publications.

Uretsky, E. (2016). *Occupational hazards sex, business, and HIV in post-Mao China*. Stanford: Stanford University Press.

Wacquant, L. (1995). Pugs at work: Bodily capital and bodily labor among professional boxers. *Body and Society, 1*, 65–93.

Walklate, S. (1991). Victims, crime prevention and social control. In R. Reiner & M. Cross (Eds.), *Beyond law and order* (pp. 204–22). Leiden: Springer.

Walklate, S. (1997). Risk and criminal victimization: A modernist dilemma? *British Journal of Criminology, 37*, 35–45.

Warhurst, C., & Nickson, D. (2009). "Who's got the look?" Emotional, aesthetic and sexualized labor in interactive services. *Gender, Work & Organization, 16*(3), 385–404. http://dx.doi.org/10.1111/j.1468-0432.2009.00450.x

Watson, R.S., & Ebrey, P.B. (Eds.). (1991). *Marriage and inequality in Chinese society* (Vol. 12). Berkeley: University of California Press.

Wu, J. (2007, March 1). New law to abolish *laojiao* system. *China Daily*, 200.

Wu, H.H. (1992). *Laogai: The Chinese Gulag* (T. Slingerland, Trans.). Boulder, CO: Westview.

Wu, H.H., & Vecsey, G. (1996). *Troublemaker: One man's crusade against China's cruelty*. London: Chatto & Windus.

Wyrod, R. (2008). Between women's rights and men's authority: Masculinity and shifting discourses of gender difference in urban Uganda. *Gender and Society, 22*(6), 799–823

Xiao, S. (2011). The "second-wife" phenomenon and the relational construction of class-coded masculinities in contemporary China. *Men and Masculinities, 14*(5), 607–27.

Yan, Y.X. (2009). *The individualization of Chinese society*. Oxford: Berg.

Yan, Y. (2010). The Chinese path to individualization. *British Journal of Sociology*, *61*(3), 489–512.

Zelizer, V. (2005). *The purchase of intimacy*. Princeton: Princeton University Press.

Zhang, L. (2014). *Thirty years of China's "custody and education"*. Retrieved August 18, 2018, from http://www.china.org.cn/china/2014-07/03/content_32848663.htm

Zhang, Y.H. (2015). *The impotence epidemic: Men's medicine and sexual desire in contemporary China*. Durham, NC: Duke University Press.

Zheng, T. (2003). Consumption, body image, and rural-urban apartheid in contemporary China. *City and Society*, *40*(2), 143–63.

Zheng, T. (2006). Cool masculinity: Male clients' sex consumption and business alliance in urban China's sex industry. *Journal of Contemporary China*, *15*(46), 161–82.

Zheng, T. (2008). Complexity of life and resistance: Informal networks of rural migrant karaoke bar hostesses in urban China's sex industry. *China: An International Journal*, *6*(1), 69–95.

Zheng, T. (2009). *Red lights: The lives of sex workers in postsocialist China*. Minneapolis: University of Minnesota Press.

Ziarek, E.P. (2008). Bare life on strike: Notes on the biopolitics of race and gender. *South Atlantic Quarterly*, *107*, 89–105.

Zinn, J.O. (2015). Towards a better understanding of risk-taking: Key concepts, dimensions and perspectives. *Health, Risk & Society*, *17*(2), 99–114.

Index

abuse, 11, 16, 39, 107, 132, 142, 144–5, 161; domestic, 47; physical and verbal, 47; police, 133; sexual, 24, 28, 42; verbal, 36, 42, 47. *See also* bullying; harassment
adaptive behaviours, 10
administrative: detention systems, 13; penalties, 123
aesthetic labour, 101
affection, 83. *See also* chemistry
"Ah Chaan" ("the uneducated" or "the hayseed"), 127
AIDS. *See* HIV/AIDS; sexually transmitted diseases
alcohol intake, excessive, 56
Alipay, 150. *See also* apps
apps, 17; mobile, 81; mobile and online, 80; mobile telephone, 77; online, 80, 150
Asian femininity, 102–3

baofang, 28. *See also* VIP: rooms
baoyang (feeding), 123
bar girl, 8, 20, 25, 27, 64–5, 72, 75, 80, 85, 87, 97–8, 102–3, 116, 167, 168
bar owner, 18, 26–7, 65, 149
bartender, 6, 9, 18–9, 78, 103
beauty queen, 65

biopolitics, 129–30, 133, 168; bio-power, 143; techniques, 55; treatment, 134
bloodline (*xiemai*), 58, 67
blow job, 116, 120. *See also* oral sex
body: autonomy, 37; pleasure, 117, 128
body capital, 3, 25, 78, 93–5, 97–9, 104, 106
body work, 93–5, 97, 99–101, 104
bondage and discipline, 115. *See also* sexual activities: BDSM
bonds: communal, 152; collective, 47
bounded: authenticity, 61, 73–5, 77, 82, 87–8, 90–91, 94, 123–4; intimacy, 61; masculinity, 61, 67; phantasms, 61; rational choice, 33–4, 38–9
bragging, 27, 54, 56, 64, 67. *See also* collaborative masculinity
breadwinner, 27, 34, 44, 55
breast enlargements, 23, 99, 100. *See also* plastic surgery
brothels, 21
bullying, 136, 143

cadres, 71, 72, 80, 89, 98, 105–6, 140, 146, 152–3; political elites, 48
camps, labour, 11, 16, 107, 121, 131, 134, 135, 136, 139, 146. *See also*